WONDROUS WOMAN

Spanish for Childbirth

Copyright © 1996, 2003, 2012 by Susan Nadathur
All rights reserved. No part of this book may be reproduced or transmitted in any form or by any means, electronic or mechanical, including photocopying, recording, or by any information storage and retrieval system, without permission in writing from the publisher. Please do not participate in or encourage piracy of copyrighted materials in violation of the author's rights.

Published in the United States of America
November 2012 by Azahar Books

Cover Design by Natalia Rivera
Cover Photo ©Nina Vaclavova
Back Cover Photo ©Nina Vaclavova
Mother with Baby Photo © Anna Omelchenko
Stock Photos provided by Dreamstime.com

For information about the author, please visit:
www.susannadathur.com

For information about workshops associated with this book:
www.crossculturalencounters.com
888-251-4562 (toll free)

ISBN-13: 978-0615693170
ISBN-10: 0615693172

This book is dedicated to all the wonderful health care professionals who make a difference in women's lives.

Communication and Culture for Healthcare Professionals

A six-part series by Susan Nadathur

Culture and Care
Spanish for Health Care Services

Expectant Mom
Spanish for Childbirth

Fragile Life
Spanish for Mother, Infant & Neonatal Care

Help Me!
Spanish for Emergency Care

Precious Child
Spanish for Pediatric Care

Wondrous Woman
Spanish for Childbirth and Women's Health

Acknowledgments

I wish to express my appreciation to the following individuals for their help and inspiration in the development of this publication.

To my parents, Paul and Louise Lostocco, who gave me the freedom and education to develop as an individual and as a professional.

To my husband, Govind Nadathur, for his constant support, patience, and loving encouragement.

To my daughter, Sita Nadathur, whose birth was the inspiration for this work.

And to the following individuals, I would like to express my gratitude for their professional input in the development and correction of this publication.

To Judy O'Connor, RN for her expert review of the manuscript. To Ivette Belén, RN, Aracelis Vega, RN, Laura Sánchez, and Claudia López for their meticulous correction of Spanish grammar, word usage, and structure. To Mmadu Onyeuwa for his help with the audio recordings and for the use of his original compositions. And to all the eager students who first used this book, helping to refine its content and give it credibility. Your input and correction have been invaluable. Thanks to you all!

Table of Contents
Prenatal Care

Greetings and Introduction	14-15
Record Keeping	16-17
Social/Family Histories	18-20
Menstrual History	21-22
Obstetric History	23-27
The Prenatal Examination	28-31
Language Activities	32-38
Cultural Reading	39-45

Childbirth Education

Common Aches and Pains	46-50
General Advice	51-54
Diet and Nutrition	55-59
Stages of Labor	60-68
Language Activities	69-73
Cultural Reading	74-79

At The Birth Center

Admissions	81-86
Initial Preparation	87-89
Labor and Delivery	90-94
Medications in Labor	95-96
Cesarean Delivery	97-99
Reaching Out To The Father	100-101
Language Activities	102-106
Cultural Reading	107-113

Mother/Infant Care and Postpartum Recovery

Initial Recovery and Newborn Assessment	116-119
Discharge Instructions	120-129
Benefits of Breastfeeding	130-131
Nursing Your Baby	132-135
Suggestions for Successful Breastfeeding	136-138
Alleviating Common Breast Discomforts	140-141
Language Activities	142-149
Cultural Reading	150-156

Neonatal Intensive Care

Communicating with the Parents	158-162
Introduction to the Unit	163-167
Care of your Baby in NICU	168-177
Common Neonatal Medical Problems	178-181
Taking your Baby Home	182-183
Language Activities	184-187
Cultural Reading	188-192

Well Woman Care and Gynecology

Family Planning and Contraception	194-195
Options in Birth Control	196-203
The STD Interview	204-207
Gynecological Cancer Screening	208-212
Menopause	213-216
Language Activities	217-223
Cultural Reading	224-229

PREFACE

Hospitals and clinics nationwide are struggling with the challenge to bridge language barriers effectively. And while there are many foreign languages being spoken in the United States today, the one presenting the most sense of urgency is Spanish, a language that will be spoken by an estimated 24.5 % of the population of the United States by the year 2050.

In order to meet the critical need for communication in health care, many providers are relying on interpreters or advising patients to bring friends or family members with them to translate. Reliance on interpreters and family members is complicating care giving in many ways. Family interpreters may not translate messages accurately, for fear of the impact on the patient or depending on whether or not they desire the person to be hospitalized. Translation by family members, and particularly children, may be further limited by the member's unfamiliarity with medical terminology and their discomfort discussing certain medical conditions, especially in the areas of women's health.

Many nurses have already observed the limitations of using interpreters and family members in the provision of care. The confidence that is needed to obtain an accurate and complete exchange of information between a nurse and her patient is often lost in the three-way relationship between a nurse, the interpreter, and her client.

The most desirable interaction between a client and her caregiver is one free of language and cultural barriers. The **Communication and Culture for Health Care Professionals** series was developed to meet the growing need for practical materials to teach health care professionals to communicate on their own in Spanish. The series was designed with the adult learner in mind, taking into consideration the unique requirements of this particular group.

Each title includes the Spanish/English terminology that health care professionals encounter most frequently on their jobs, supported by a variety of language activities, grammar explanations, and cultural readings. Each title is accompanied by an audio program which follows the text and provides models for correct pronunciation as well as numerous opportunities for oral practice.

Wondrous Woman is an introductory program designed especially for childbirth and women's health care professionals. The program is appropriate for those with no previous language background as well as for those who have some background in Spanish but are unfamiliar with the specific terminology particular to women's health care.

A practical orientation ensures that students will quickly acquire sufficient communicative skills to improve the quality of care they provide their clients in a women's health care setting. Basic grammar and practical terminology are combined in a communicative approach that will encourage learners to use the language in a meaningful manner.

All of the chapters are organized around the following key features to facilitate the learning process and guide the learner from simple vocabulary to more complex phrases, to the ultimate goal of communication in a meaningful, situational context.

- **Key Terminology**: Phrases, questions and instructions specific to content area are provided in this section, offering the learner linguistic content which is directly relevant to her professional orientation and learning goals.

- **Targeted Grammar and Structure**: Grammar is presented in a health care context and is merged progressively with health care terminology in various medical settings.

- **Language Activities**: Designed to lead the learner toward the ultimate goal of creative communication in Spanish. The student will internalize new material, personalize what has been acquired, and then through role playing, interview, and other activities, use the language in meaningful communication.

- **Cultural Notes**: Brief readings that focus on issues of cultural interest to the health care community, discussed in the context of how these issues may be creating misunderstanding and conflict in the workplace. The purpose of this section is to raise consciousness of cultural differences and taboos, and through this new understanding, achieve acceptance.

When used in conjunction with the audio program, **Wondrous Woman** offers a balanced approach to learning the language necessary to communicate with Spanish-speaking patients in a women's health care setting. At the same time, students will gain awareness of the nature of interpersonal relationships and of the rich cultural heritage of Latino groups residing in the United States today.

As this publication is designed for use by health professionals nationwide, the author has tried to choose words that will be understood by most Spanish speakers. Because of regional differences in the way the language is spoken, however, the learner may encounter slight variations in pronunciation, word choice and structure among the various Latino communities now residing in the United States. The text has been tested in Mexican, Puerto Rican, and other Latin American communities to assure accuracy and appropriateness of the vocabulary and terminology being utilized.

Learning a foreign language is a tremendous challenge, but it is also a great accomplishment. Spanish is a lively, vibrant language. Learn to speak it and to enjoy those who come from Spanish-speaking cultures. Crossing cultural and language barriers is not always easy, but the depth of human understanding and compassion for others that results is a life-changing force. Cross cultural understanding is a gift we can share with each other.

Unit One
PRENATAL CARE VISITS

Greetings and Introductions
Record Keeping
Social and Family Histories
Menstrual History
Past Pregnancies and Deliveries
Medical History
The Prenatal Examination
Formal and Informal You (Usted vs. Tú)
The Future Perfect Tense and Prenatal Care
American Nurses/Latina Clients

PRENATAL CARE VISITS
Greetings and Introductions

1. Good day.
Buenos días.

2. Good afternoon.
Buenas tardes.

3. Good evening.
Buenas noches.

4. I am Ana,
Soy Ana,

5. your nurse, midwife, doctor, receptionist, secretary.
su enfermera, partera, doctor (a), recepcionista, secretaria.

6. What is your name?
¿Cómo se llama usted?

7. How are you today?
¿Cómo está usted hoy?

8. Do you speak English?
¿Habla inglés?

9. Do you understand English?
¿Entiende inglés?

10. I speak little Spanish.
Hablo poco español.

11. Please speak slowly.
Por favor, hable despacio.

12. Answer with "yes" or "no".
Conteste con "sí" o "no."

13. I don't understand.
No entiendo.

PRENATAL CARE VISITS
Record Keeping

1. Do you have an appointment?
¿Tiene cita?

2. What's your name? Last name? Second last name?
¿Cuál es su nombre? ¿Apellido? ¿Segundo apellido?

3. Do you have a record here?
¿Tiene record aquí?

4. What is your record number?
¿Cuál es su número de record?

5. Sit down, please.
Siéntese, por favor.

6. Fill out this form.
Llene el formulario.

7. The form is in Spanish.
El formulario está en español.

8. Do you read Spanish? English?
¿Lee español? ¿inglés?

9. Do you have insurance? Medicaid?
¿Tiene plan médico? ¿Medicaid?

10. Have you applied for Medicaid?
¿Ha solicitado Medicaid?

11. Who is the principal person insured?
¿Quién es el asegurado principal?

12. What is this person's relationship to the patient?
¿Cuál es la relación de esta persona a la paciente?

13. Please give me your card.
Deme su tarjeta, por favor.

14. Your co-payment is six dollars.
Su co-pago es seis dólares.

15. Your insurance has a two-dollar deductible.
Su plan tiene un deducible de dos dólares.

16. Sign here.
Firme aquí.

17. Wait here.
Espere aquí.

18. The doctor will see you soon.
El doctor le verá pronto.

PRENATAL CARE VISITS
Obtaining a Social / Family History

1. I'm going to ask you some questions.
Le voy a hacer unas preguntas.

2. I know that these questions are very personal.
Yo sé que estas preguntas son muy personales.

3. But, they are important to your health.
Pero, son importantes para su salud.

4. Are you married? Single? Divorced? Widowed?
¿Es usted casada? ¿Soltera? ¿Divorciada? ¿Viuda?

5. Who do you live with?
¿Con quién vive usted?

6. Husband? Boyfriend? Parents? Sibling? Grandparents? Aunt/Uncle? Friend?
¿Esposo? ¿Novio? ¿Padres? ¿Hermanos? ¿Abuelos? ¿Tíos? ¿Amigos?

7. Do you work? Where?
¿Trabaja usted? ¿Dónde?

8. Do you work with chemicals?
¿Trabaja con químicos?

9. Does your husband work? Where?

¿Trabaja su esposo? ¿Dónde?

10. How old are you?
¿Cuántos años tiene usted?

11. What is your nationality?
¿Cuál es su nacionalidad?

12. Have you been pregnant before?
¿Ha estado embarazada antes?

13. How many times?
¿Cuántas veces?

14. Did you receive prenatal care?
¿Recibió cuidado prenatal?

15. How many children do you have?
¿Cuántos hijos tiene usted?

16. Any twins? Triplets?
¿Gemelos? (en Puerto Rico) ¿Guates? (en México) ¿Trillizos?

17. Is there a history of birth defects in your family? Genetic abnormalities?
¿Hay historial de defectos de nacimiento en su familia? ¿anormalidades genéticas?

18. Was anyone born with mental retardation? Down's Syndrome?
¿Nació alguien con retraso mental? ¿Mongolismo?

19. Do you take any medication? Illegal drugs?
¿Toma algún medicamento? ¿Drogas ilegales?

20. Do you drink alcohol? Coffee?
¿Toma alcohol? ¿Café?

21. How much? One cup? Two beers? Three glasses of wine?
¿Cuánto? ¿Una taza? ¿Dos cervezas? ¿Tres vasos de vino?

22. Do you smoke? Cigarettes? Marijuana?
¿Fuma? ¿Cigarillos? ¿Marijuana?

23. How much? A pack a day? Two packs?
¿Cuánto? ¿Un paquete al día? ¿Dos paquetes?

24. Have you gained or lost weight recently?
¿Ha aumentado o bajado de peso recientemente?

25. How much did you weigh before you became pregnant?
¿Cuánto pesaba antes de quedar embarazada?

26. What is your present weight?
¿Cuál es su peso actual?

27. Have you had suicidal thoughts?
¿Ha pensado alguna vez en suicidarse (matarse)?

28. Have you been depressed?
¿Ha estado deprimida?

PRENATAL CARE VISITS
Obtaining a Menstrual History

1. How old were you when you began to menstruate?
¿A qué edad empezó a menstruar?

2. When was the first day of your last menstrual cycle?
¿Cuándo fue el primer día de su última menstruación?

3. Was it normal?
¿Fue normal?

4. Do you have pain/cramping with your period?
¿Tiene dolor / calambres cuando baja la menstruación?

5. How many days does your period last?
¿Cuántos días le dura la menstruación?

6. Is the flow heavy or light?
¿Sangra mucho o poco?

7. How many pads/tampons do you use a day?
¿Cuántos toallas sanitarias / cuántos tampones usa al día?

8. How often does your period come?
¿Cada cuántos días le viene la menstruación?

9. Is it usually regular? Early? Late?
¿Normalmente es regular? ¿Adelantada? ¿Atrasada?

10. Do you ever miss your period?
¿Le ha faltado alguna vez la menstruación?

11. Do you spot between periods?
¿Sangra entre las menstruaciones?

12. Have you had a period in the last month?
¿Ha tenido una menstruación en el último mes?

PRENATAL CARE VISITS
Obtaining an Obstetric History

Past Pregnancies/Deliveries

1. Have you had any problems with past pregnancies?
¿Ha tenido algún problema en sus embarazos previos?

2. Were all your pregnancies term?
¿Llegaron a las cuarenta semanas todos sus embarazos?

3. Have you ever had a spontaneous abortion?
¿Ha tenido un aborto natural?

4. Have you ever had a therapeutic abortion?
¿Ha tenido un aborto provocado?

5. How far along were you when you lost the baby?
¿Cuánto tiempo tenía al perder el bebé?

6. Did you receive medical treatment?
¿Recibió tratamiento médico?

7. Have you ever had a stillborn baby?
¿Ha tenido un niño que nació muerto?

8. Have you ever had a premature baby?
¿Ha tenido un niño que nació prematuro?

9. How many months was he/she at birth?
¿Cuántos meses tenía al nacer?

10. Have you had any problems with past deliveries?
¿Ha tenido algún problema en sus partos previos?

11. Hemorrhaging? High blood pressure? Toxemia? Placenta Previa?
¿Hemorragia? ¿Presión alta? ¿Toxemia? ¿Placenta Previa?

12. Have you ever had a cesarean birth?
¿Ha tenido una cesárea?

13. Have you ever had a breech birth?
¿Ha tenido un parto de nalgas?

14. Have you ever had a baby born with the cord wrapped around his neck?
¿Ha tenido un bebé que nació con el cordón enredado al cuello?

15. Have you ever had a forceps delivery?
¿Ha tenido un parto con fórceps?

16. Did you receive anesthesia during labor?
¿Recibió anestesia durante algún parto?

17. What was the duration of your longest (shortest) labor?
¿Cuánto duró su parto más largo (más corto)?

18. What was the weight of your largest (smallest) baby at birth?
¿Cúanto pesó su bebé más grande (más pequeño) al nacer?

Medical History

1. Have you ever had diabetes during pregnancy?
¿Ha tenido diabetes durante algún embarazo?

2. Have you ever had high blood pressure?
¿Ha tenido la presión alta?

3. Have you ever had anemia?
¿Ha tenido anemia?

4. Have you ever had a bladder infection?
¿Ha tenido una infección de la vejiga?

5. Have you ever had a vaginal infection?
¿Ha tenido una infección vaginal?

6. Have you ever had frequent urinary track infections?
¿Ha tenido infecciones frecuentes de orina?

7. Have you ever had problems with your uterus, ovaries or tubes?
¿Ha tenido problemas con la matriz, los ovarios o las trompas?

8. Have you ever had a breast tumor or cyst?
¿Ha tenido tumor o quiste en los senos?

9. Have you ever had varicose veins?
¿Ha tenido venas varicosas?

10. Have you ever had surgery?
¿Ha tenido cirugía?

11. Have you ever had a venereal or sexually-transmitted disease?
¿Ha tenido una enfermedad venérea o sexualmente transmitido?

12. Have you ever had a blood transfusion?
¿Ha tenido una transfusión de sangre?

13. Have you had vaginal bleeding?
¿Ha tenido sangrado vaginal?

14. Were there clots?
¿Hubieron coágulos?

15. How much bleeding was there? A cup? A tablespoon? A teaspoon?
¿Cuánto sangrado hubo? ¿Un vaso? ¿Una cucharada? ¿Una cucharadita?

16. Did you have to use a sanitary pad or a tampon?
¿Tuvo que usar una toalla sanitaria o un tampón?

17. How often did you have to change it?
¿Cada cuánto tuvo que cambiarlo?

18. How long did it last?
¿Cuánto duró?

19. Have you had any vaginal discharge?
¿Ha tenido flujo (descarga) vaginal?

20. Has the discharge changed?
¿Ha cambiado el flujo (la descarga)?

21. Does it have a bad odor?
¿Tiene mal olor?

22. Is the discharge white, gray, clear, or yellow?
¿Es el flujo (la descarga) de color blanco, gris, claro o amarillo?

23. Is it thick or thin?
¿Es espeso o líquido?

24. Does it burn? Itch?
¿Le arde? ¿Le pica?

PRENATAL CARE VISITS
The Prenatal Examination

1. Step on the scale.
Súbase a la báscula (en México) / la balanza (en Puerto Rico).

2. I need a urine sample.
Necesito una muestra de orina.

3. Go to the bathroom.
Vaya al baño.

4. Leave the cup on the counter.
Deje el recipiente en el mostrador.

5. Take off your clothes from the waist down.
Quítese la ropa de la cintura para abajo.

6. Take off all your clothes.
Quítese toda la ropa.

7. Put on the gown.
Póngase la bata.

8. Sit on the table.
Siéntese en la mesa.

9. I need to take your blood pressure.
Necesito tomarle la presión de sangre.

10. I am going to listen to the baby's heartbeat.
Voy a escuchar los latidos del corazón del bebé.

11. Is your baby moving?
¿Se mueve el bebé?

12. I'm going to examine you.
Le voy a examinar.

13. Don't be afraid.
No tenga miedo.

14. You will feel less discomfort if you relax.
Sentirá menos molestias si se relaja.

15. First, I am going to examine your breasts.
Primero, voy a examinarle los senos.

16. Lie down, please.
Acuéstese, por favor.

17. Raise your arm over your head.
Levante el brazo sobre la cabeza.

18. Now I am going to begin the pelvic exam.
Ahora voy a iniciar el examen pélvico.

19. Put your feet here.
Ponga los pies aquí.

20. Separate your legs.
Separe las piernas.

21. Relax.
Relájese.

22. I´m going to insert the speculum in your vagina.
Voy a introducir el espéculo en la vagina.

23. The speculum is an instrument that dilates the vaginal opening.
El espéculo es un instrumento que dilata la abertura vaginal.

24. I am going to insert it slowly to avoid discomfort.
Lo voy a insertar poco a poco para que no sienta molestia.

25. Tell me if you feel pain.
Dígame si siente dolor.

26. I am going to take a sample from the lining of the cervix for a Pap Smear.
Le voy a tomar una muestra del tejido cervical para la prueba Papanicolau.

27. We will test this sample for cancer.
Analizaremos la muestra para cáncer.

28. Now I am slowly going to remove the speculum.
Ahora voy a retirar gradualmente el espéculo.

29. Now I am going to check your uterus and ovaries.
Ahora voy a examinarle el útero y los ovarios.

30. I will examine you with my fingers.
Le examinaré con mis dedos.

31. I am going to feel the neck of the uterus to determine its consistency, form and position.
Voy a sentir el cuello uterino para determinar su consistencia, forma, y posición.

32. Now I am going to measure your pelvis.
Ahora le voy a medir la pelvis.

33. We are finished.
Ya terminamos.

34. You may get dressed.
Puede vestirse.

PRENATAL CARE VISITS
Language Activities and Study Guide

Instructions: Set your own timeframe for the following activities. It is recommended that a beginning learner allow three months for this unit, dedicating approximately 30 minutes a day to the goal of learning Spanish for prenatal care.

Unit 1 Begin Date: _____
Projected End Date: _____

A. Key Phrases

Listen to the phrases presented on pages 14-31 on the audio program. These phrases will help you to obtain medical and family histories as well as allow you to be able to guide a woman through a pelvic examination in Spanish. Repeat each phrase after the instructor in Spanish. Listen for the vocabulary you already know. This will give you confidence as you begin to recognize familiar words. When you are confident of the pronunciation, read the phrases into a recorder. Replay your recording and listen for any errors in pronunciation.

B. Targeted Grammar and Structure:
Formal & Informal You

The subject pronouns *"tú"* and *"usted"* both mean "you" in Spanish. *"Tú"* is usually used with someone with whom you are on a first-name basis and with a child. *"Usted"* is used with all others and conveys a message of respect. Using *"usted"* where *"tú"* is normally used may seem stiff and overly formal or make more obvious the fact that you are not a native speaker, but it will not offend anyone. Using *"tú"* where *"usted"* would be proper may offend someone if the user is a native Spanish speaker. The error is understood, however, and would not be considered offensive from a non-Spanish speaker.

Certain ethnic groups (Puerto Ricans for example) use the *"tú"* form more readily than other groups. And in some situations, for example during labor and delivery or with the intention of establishing confidence with a patient, it is sometimes recommended to use the *"tú"* form, even if you do not know your client well. This form can establish trust and intimacy where the formal *"usted"* may form a barrier. It is always best, however, to use the *"usted"* form when in doubt, and let the relationship determine the formality of speech.

C. Targeted Grammar and Structure:

The Future Perfect Tense

In this section you will learn how to ask questions appropriate for prenatal assessment. One way to ask questions in Spanish is to use a verb tense called the *Future Perfect*. This tense allows you to ask about events that began in the past and continue in the future. It translates to the English *Have you + Past Participle*. Example: Have you had?

Follow the simple rules below for constructing this tense in both the *usted* (formal you) and *tú* (informal you) forms.

Rule:

1. Use the auxiliary **ha** (usted form) or **has** (tú form) with every verb, no matter if it ends in ar, er, or ir.

   Ha or **has** translate to the English auxiliary *have* and are derived from the Spanish verb *haber*.

2. If a verb ends in **ar,** remove the **ar** and add **ado**
   Example: tom**ar** -- tom -- tom**ado**

   Add the auxiliary **ha** to form ¿**Ha tomado?** (Have you taken? **formal**) or **has** to form ¿**Has tomado?** (Have you taken? **informal**)

3. If a verb ends in **er** or **ir** remove the **er** or **ir** and add **ido**
   Example: com**er** ---- com ---- com**ido**

   Add the auxiliary **ha** to form **¿Ha comido?** (Have you eaten? **formal**) or **has** to form **¿Has comido?** (Have you eaten? **informal**)
   Example: viv**ir** ---- viv ---- viv**ido**

   Add the auxiliary **ha** to form **¿Ha vivido** (Have you lived? **formal**) or **has** to form **¿Has vivido** (Have you eaten? **informal**).

Note: Above is the rule. There are always exceptions. In Spanish you will find many irregular constructions in the present perfect tense. There is no way for you to know which verbs conjugate as irregular forms except through usage and by referring to a verb book for verification.

There is one key structure in the present perfect tense that will be used extensively in prenatal assessment of a patient´s medical history:

Ha tenido: ah. ten.ee.though: **Have you had?**

Learn this one structure well.
It is vital to communication in a health care setting.

D. Language Learning Activities

Look through the terminology presented on pages 23-27 of the text. Mark all the phrases which ask a question with *ha tenido*. Next, you will engage in a substitution activity using the present perfect tense. Write 7 **additional** questions using **ha tenido** in a prenatal situation. These questions should be pertinent to your work and ones which you use on a daily basis. Refer to the vocabulary list below for help with this exercise.

Vocabulario Especializado:
El Historial Médico

abortion: *aborto provocado*
Aids: *Sida*
anemia: *anemia*
arthritis: *artritis*
asthma: *asma*
cancer: *cáncer*
cesarean: *cesárea*
chicken pox: *varicela*
convulsiones: *convulsiones*
depression: *depresión*
epilepsy: *epilepsia*
gonnorrhea: *gonorrea*
heart attack: *ataque al corazón*
hepatitis: *hepatitis*
high blood pressure: *presión alta*
hypertension: *hipertensión*

hysterectomy: *histerectomía*
kidney disease: *enfermedad de los riñones*
liver disease: *enfermedad del hígado*
Measles: *sarampión*
Meningitis: *meningitis*
miscarriage: *aborto natural*
mumps: *paperas*
parasites: *parásitos*
pneumonia: *pulmonía*
psychiatric problems: *problemas psiquiátricos*
smallpox: *viruela*
stroke: *derrame cerebral*
syphillis: *sífilis*
tuberculosis: *tuberculosis*

¿Ha tenido . . . ?

1. _____
2. _____
3. _____
4. _____
5. _____
6. _____
7. _____

Practice your questions several times until you are comfortable with the pronunciation and the words flow smoothly. Read the questions into a recorder. Replay your recording and listen for any errors in pronunciation.

Cultural Reading
American Nurses / Latina Clients
Strategies for Cross-Cultural Understanding

Have you ever found yourself exasperated, frustrated or wondering why you just can't seem to get through to your Spanish-speaking clients, even if you communicate in their language? Do you ever feel helpless, uncomfortable and even angry when they don't follow the advice you offer or they resist answering questions about their personal and medical histories?

If you have found yourself struggling with such emotions, you have experienced what is called "culture shock." You are in conflict between the values and norms of your culture and what women from other cultures do when they are sick, in pain, or experiencing a life-changing force such as childbirth.

We all have a tendency to judge other cultures on the basis of our own culture's beliefs and values. Technically this is termed "ethnocentrism." Practically, it is what causes barriers in cross-cultural interactions between healthcare professionals and clients from different ethnic and socio-economic backgrounds.

We need to be aware of our natural tendency towards ethnocentrism, while at the same time be willing to rise above that inclination to deliver culturally-relevant health care. When in our encounters with culturally-diverse populations we can begin to widen our own perspective by exploring the values and norms of other cultures, then we have taken the first steps towards true cross-cultural understanding.

Once we recognize that conflict exists, we can then go on to acquire cultural knowledge that will serve as a tool to understanding. Begin today, right now, to overcome the challenge of culture-based patterns of behavior. Start where many of you see your Spanish-speaking clients for the first time: in the prenatal clinic or doctor's office.

One of your first interactions will be to obtain information. However, Latina women are often shy about discussing their medical and family histories. Questions about abortions, miscarriages, and stillborn children are considered extremely personal and an uncomfortable topic for discussion outside of the family.

As childbirth professionals, however, these types of questions are an important part of your job. I would encourage you to ask the questions you need to, but preface them with a reassuring statement such as: *Yo sé que éstas preguntas son muy personales.* (I know these questions are very personal). *Pero son muy importantes para su salud y la de su bebé.* (But, they are important to your health and to the health of your baby).

The Latina woman, like all women, is usually very concerned about her baby's well-being. This type of response may help her to understand better the nature of the questioning and the importance of her responses.

Another issue that often presents a stumbling block to health care providers working with Spanish-speaking clients is the tendency of Hispanic women to defer to their spouses when asked questions about their medical histories. American health care providers have been taught to direct their questions to their clients, but are often unsuccessful when following this protocol with Hispanic women.

The custom of deference to male authority figures is a part of the culture and not at all uncommon in the Hispanic community. The woman in many Latino cultures has been taught to defer to the dominant male in her life, be it her father, brother, husband or boyfriend. Sometimes, you may find that the male she has come to rely on may not be answering your questions accurately, either out of embarrassment or because he really doesn't know the answers to the intimate questions you are asking.

You may work on empowering the woman to be her own advocate, but this strategy would require combating many deeply engrained traditions. Many of the women you work with are from small villages where traditions are often hard to change.

Instead, I suggest that you empower the man. Gain him as your ally. Let him know that he has an important role to play in his wife´s care.

Say something like *Su esposa le necesita.* (Your wife needs you). *Su bebé le necesita.* (Your baby needs you). Then simply tell him to ask her the questions that he is answering for her. Say, *Pregúntele a ella, por favor.* (Ask her, please). *Es importante para ella que yo tenga esta información.* (It´s important for her that I have this information).

Remember, both the husband and wife will most likely be uncomfortable with the questions you are asking. When you ask a male to ask his partner about something personal, encourage them both to understand that you know it is a sensitive question by saying to the woman, *Perdone que le pregunte, pero. . .* (Pardon me that I ask, but . . .). This will put the husband at ease as well as he senses your sensitivity to his discomfort. Remember, both the husband and wife will be somewhat uncomfortable in this medical environment which is so familiar to you. It may be the first time either is in a medical office, whether in this country or in their own.

Also keep in mind when considering the issue of privacy that many Latin-American women find it extremely embarrassing to undergo an examination of areas that they feel are private, especially should the examination be performed by a male doctor or health-care provider. In light of this traditional concern for privacy, try to ensure that your interactions with Latin women, as with all women, are respectful, friendly and warm, and that there are measures taken to insure both dignity and privacy in all prenatal care functions and procedures.

You may reassure your client with a few kind words like *Perdone. Va a ser un poquito incómodo, pero necesito examinarle.* (I'm sorry. It's going to be a little uncomfortable, but I need to exam you). *Es importante para entender mejor el progreso de su embarazo.* (It's important to understand the progress of your pregnancy).

You may wish to ask her husband to leave the room at this time. His absence will allow her some privacy as well as afford you the opportunity to ask her a few questions if you suspect physical and/or sexual abuse. As I am sure you are aware, your client will be very reluctant to answer any questions related to abuse. If you can gain her confidence throughout a series of prenatal visits, however, you may be successful in obtaining some vital information about potential mistreatment.

Confidence and trust are two very important values that we must recognize and respect if we are to achieve successful cross-cultural interactions in the Hispanic community. In Spanish these values translate to: *personalismo* and *confianza.*

Personalismo is the value of treating a client as an individual, of knowing more about a patient than her medical history. It is knowing her as a person as opposed to a record number.

The concept of *personalismo* is as simple as asking a client about her spouse or her other children. It includes being aware of situations that are making it difficult for her to be able to make her appointment, such as lack of transportation or an inflexible work schedule. It is knowing her as a person, and she knowing you beyond the professional role you represent. Courtesy and small talk are important in the Hispanic culture. If you take a personal interest in your client, and allow her to get to know you, you will have a much more positive interaction because you will have established *confianza*.

Confianza is mutual trust and respect earned through genuine interest in the well-being, language limitations, and cultural individuality of a client. It means learning the language and not relying on an interpreter as you wait impassively for a translation of your patient's concerns. *Confianza* is built on the small attempts you make to get to know your patient. It builds on something as simple as "How are you today," spoken in her language. Once you begin to try to cross that cultural and language barrier, you will touch her life as well as enrich your own. *Confianza* is guaranteed when you relate to your client as a person, in her language, and not as a number. And when you earn that *confianza*, compliance is assured. Your patient will begin to express her feelings, listen more carefully, and be more likely to follow the advice you offer. She will want to because she trusts you. Once you decide to cross culture and language barriers, you will touch lives, and in the process, change your own.

Questions for Discussion

1. What experiences in your professional life have you had with "culture shock?"

2. What cultural values do you hold which differ from those of Hispanic clients with whom you have worked?

3. What strategies can you implement to put a patient more at ease in a formal medical setting?

4. What are two important values to the Hispanic culture that we must recognize and respect in order to achieve successful cross-cultural interactions in health care?

5. What is often the result of having achieved *confianza* with a Spanish-speaking patient?

Unit Two
PRENATAL CARE VISITS

Practical Remedies for Common Aches & Pains
Offering General Prenatal Advice
Diet and Nutrition
First Stage of Labor (Effacement)
First Stage of Labor (Dilation)
First Stage of Labor (Transition)
Second Stage of Labor (Delivery)
Third Stage of Labor (Delivery of the Placenta)
Forming Commands & Delivering Instructions
Forming Questions in Spanish
Non-compliance in Prenatal Health Care

CHILDBIRTH EDUCATION
Practical Remedies for Common Aches and Pains

Low Back Pain
(Dolores en la parte baja de la espalda)

1. Keep your back straight and your head up.
Mantenga la espalda recta y la cabeza en alto.

2. Wear comfortable, low-heeled shoes.
Use calzado cómodo y de tacón bajo.

3. Do daily prenatal exercises.
Haga ejercicios prenatales diariamente.

Leg Cramps
(Calambres en las Piernas)

1. Be sure to have enough calcium in your diet.
Asegúrese de que tenga en su dieta suficiente calcio.

2. Take a warm bath before going to bed.
Báñese en agua tibia antes de acostarse.

3. Do exercises to stretch the calves.
Haga ejercicios para estirar los músculos de las pantorrillas.

4. Massage the cramped muscles.
Hágase masajes en los músculos acalambrados.

Varicose Veins
(Venas Varicosas)

1. Avoid crossing your legs.
Evite cruzar las piernas.

2. Avoid standing for long periods of time.
Evite estar de pie por mucho tiempo.

3. Rest your legs in an elevated position.
Descanse los pies en una posición elevada.

4. Walk to promote circulation.
Camine para fomentar la circulación.

Shortness of Breath
(Falta de Aire)

1. Practice deep chest breathing.
Practique la respiración profunda del pecho.

2. Lift your arms over your head and stretch.
Levante los brazos sobre la cabeza y estírese.

Heartburn
(Acidez)

1. Eat more frequent, smaller meals.
Coma con más frecuencia porciones pequeñas de comida.

2. Avoid greasy and spicy foods.
Evite los alimentos grasientos o con muchas especias.

3. Drink milk, mineral water or yogurt when acidity begins.
Tome leche, agua mineral o yogurt cuando sienta acidez.

Nausea and Vomiting
(Náuseas y Vómitos)

1. Before getting out of bed, eat salty crackers.
Antes de salir de la cama, coma galletas saladas.

2. Get out of bed slowly and avoid rapid movement.
Levántese de la cama lentamente y evite movimientos repentinos.

3. Drink tea or carbonated water.
Tome té o agua carbonatada.

4. Get some fresh air.
Tome aire fresco.

Constipation
(Estreñimiento)

1. Drink from eight to ten glasses of fluids daily.
Tome de ocho a diez vasos de líquido diariamente.

2. Eat more fruits, vegetables, grains and cereals.
Coma más frutas, vegetales, granos y cereales.

3. Don´t use laxatives.
No use laxantes.

Fatigue
(Cansancio)

1. Take short naps during the day.
Tome pequeñas siestas durante el día

2. Have your doctor check for anemia.
Pida a su doctor que compruebe si tiene anemia.

Headaches
(Dolores de Cabeza)

1. Relax and rest.
Relájese y descanse.

2. Gradually reduce your consumption of caffeine.
Reduzca gradualmente su consumo de cafeína.

Vaginal Discharge
(Flujo / Descarga Vaginal)

1. Avoid wearing tight pants.
Evite usar pantalones apretados.

2. Wear cotton rather than synthetic underwear.
Use ropa interior de algodón en vez de fibras sintéticas.

3. Take a daily bath or shower.
Tome una ducha o baño diariamente.

Hemorrhoids
(Hemorroides)

1. Use an icepack to soothe the affected area.
Use una bolsa con hielo para calmar el dolor.

2. Soak a gauze pad with witch hazel and hold it against the hemorrhoids for twenty minutes.
*Empape una gasa con hamamelis y manténgala
Sobre las hemorroides por veinte minutos.*

Breast Discomforts
(Malestares de los Senos)

1. Wear a supportive bra.
Use un sostén que soporte con firmeza.

2. Wear a cotton rather than synthetic bra.
Use un sostén de algodón en vez de fibras sintéticas.

CHILDBIRTH EDUCATION
Offering General Advice

Prenatal care is important to . . .
El cuidado prenatal es importante para . . .

1. assure good health for you and your baby.
 asegurar la salud de usted y su bebé.

2. identify and manage conditions which may cause problems for you and your baby.
identificar y manejar condiciones que puedan ocasionar problemas para usted y su bebé.

3. reduce the risk of a premature or underweight baby, and birth defects.
reducir el riesgo de un bebé prematuro, de poco peso y con defectos de nacimiento.

Your Part in Prenatal Care . . .
Su Parte en el Cuidado Prenatal . . .

4. Keep your appointments and heed the advice of your doctor or nurse.
Cumple con sus citas y lleve a cabo los consejos de su doctor o enfermera.

5. Encourage your partner to attend medical visits with you.
Anime a su pareja a que atienda a las visitas médicas con usted.

6. Learn all you can about your pregnancy.
Aprenda todo lo que pueda sobre su embarazo.

7. Ask questions of your doctor and nurse.
Haga preguntas a su doctor o enfermera.

8. Go to childbirth education classes.
Vaya a clases prenatales.

9. Do preparatory exercises for labor.
Haga ejercicios preparatorios para el parto.

10. Avoid strenuous exercise.
Evite los ejercicios fuertes.

11. Rest as much as possible.
Descanse mucho.

12. Try to sleep eight hours a night.
Trate de dormir ocho horas cada noche.

13. Try to maintain a regular schedule for sleeping.
Trate de mantener un horario regular para dormir.

14. Don't smoke. Stop smoking.
No fume. Deje de fumar.

15. If you can't stop smoking, try to smoke less.
Si no puede dejar de fumar, trate de fumar menos.

16. Smoking can cause premature and low birth-weight babies.
El fumar puede causar bebés prematuros, o bebés que nacen de poco peso.

17. Smoking can cause miscarriage and stillborn babies.
El fumar puede causar el aborto espontáneo y el nacimiento de feto muerto.

18. Don't drink alcoholic beverages.
No tome bebidas alcohólicas.

19. Alcohol is dangerous to you and your baby.
El alcohol es dañino para usted y su bebé.

20. It can cause vaginal bleeding and premature detachment of the placenta.
Puede causar sangrado vaginal y desprendimiento prematuro de la placenta.

21. It can cause your baby to be born with birth defects.
Puede causar que se bebé nazca con defectos de nacimiento.

22. Don´t take any medications without consulting with your doctor.
No tome ninguna medicina sin consultar a su doctor.

23. Don´t take any illegal drugs.
No tome ninguna droga ilegal.

24. Illegal drugs may cause spontaneous addiction of your baby.
Las drogas ilegales le pueden causar adicción espontáneo a su bebé.

25. Cocaine may cause slow development of the brain and/or brain damage.
La cocaína puede causar un desarrollo lento del cerebro y/o daño cerebral.

CHILDBIRTH EDUCATION
Diet and Nutrition/The WIC Interview

1. Have you received assistance from WIC before?
¿Ha recibido ayuda de WIC antes?

2. Did you bring a check stub? light or water bill?
¿Trajo su comprobante de ingreso? ¿factura de luz o agua?

3. What did you eat yesterday for breakfast? lunch? dinner? snack?
¿Qué comió ayer para el desayuno? ¿el almuerzo? ¿la cena? ¿la merienda?

4. How much did you eat?
¿Cuánto comió?

5. How was the meal cooked? Fried? Boiled? Baked?
¿Cómo estaba preparada la comida? ¿Frita? ¿Hervida? ¿Al horno?

6. What did you drink?
¿Qué tomó?

7. Have you eaten today?
¿Comió hoy?

8. Have you had any food cravings?
¿Le ha dado algunos antojos?

9. Have you had decreased appetite?
¿Ha disminuido el apetito?

10. Do you have a healthy appetite?
¿Tiene buen apetito?

11. Do you have any food allergies?
¿Tiene alergia a alguna comida?

12. You need to gain weight.
Usted necesita aumentar de peso.

13. A weight gain of between 25-35 pounds is normal during pregnancy.
Un aumento de peso entre veinticinco a treinta y cinco libras es normal durante el embarazo.

14. Gaining weight during pregnancy is not the same as getting fat.
El aumento de peso durante el embarazo no es lo mismo que engordar.

15. This increase in weight is good for your baby´s development.
Ese aumento de peso es bueno para el desarrollo de su bebé.

16. You need to control your weight gain.
Usted necesita controlar su aumento de peso.

17. Eat nutritious foods.
Coma alimentos nutritivos.

18. Eat foods high in protein, calcium, vitamins and iron.
Coma alimentos altos en proteínas, calcio, vitaminas, y hierro.

19. Eat eggs, cheese, fish and dried grains (beans).
Coma huevos, queso, pescado y granos secos (habichuelas).

20. Eat a lot of fruits and vegetables.
Coma muchas frutas y vegetales.

21. Drink four glasses of milk a day.
Tome cuatro vasos de leche diariamente.

22. Drink low fat instead of whole milk.
Tome la leche baja en grasa en lugar de la leche completa.

23. You can substitute cheese for milk as a source of calcium.
Puede sustituir el queso por la leche como fuente de calcio.

24. Drink juice enriched with Vitamin C.
Tome jugo enriquecido con Vitamina C.

25. Eat three meals a day.
Coma tres comidas al día.

26. Eat moderate but adequate amounts.
Coma cantidades moderadas pero adecuadas.

27. If you are hungry in between meals, eat a fresh fruit.
Si le da hambre entre comidas, coma una fruta fresca.

28. Eat a healthy breakfast.
Coma un desayuno saludable.

29. Prepare meats in the oven or cooked with little fat.
Prepare las carnes al horno o guisadas con poca grasa.

30. Choose lean meats.
Escoja carnes magras.

31. Cut off any visible fat from meat before cooking.
Recorte cualquier grasa visible antes de cocinar.

32. Use little salt in food preparations.
Use poca sal en la preparación de las comidas.

33. Avoid salty foods like sausage, hot dogs and french fries.
Evite alimentos muy salados como salchichón, salchichas, y papitas fritas.

34. Avoid fried foods.
Evite las frituras.

35. Avoid excess fat when cooking beans.
Evite el exceso de grasa al guisar los frijoles.

36. Don't eat raw meat or fish, like ceviche.
No coma ni carne ni pescado crudo (como el ceviche).

37 Avoid sweets like cake, cookies and ice cream.
Evite los dulces como el bizcocho, las galletas y el helado.

38 Avoid carbonated beverages and malts.
Evite las bebidas carbonatadas y las maltas.

39. Avoid sugared beverages, like fruit punches.
Evite las bebidas azucaradas, como los ponches de fruta.

40. Drink 6 to 8 glasses of water daily.
Tome seis a ocho vasos de agua diariamente.

41. Avoid caffeine. It can make you nervous.
Evite la cafeína. Puede ponerle nerviosa.

42. There is caffeine in Coca-Cola, tea, chocolate and coffee.
Hay cafeína en la Coca-Cola, el té, el chocolate y el café.

43. Take prenatal vitamins / iron pills / a multivitamin daily.
Tome vitaminas prenatales / pastillas de hierro / una multivitamina diariamente.

CHILDBIRTH EDUCATION
First Stage: Labor

Effacement
(El Borramiento)

1. These are the first hours of labor.
Son las primeras horas del trabajo de parto.

2. It is the longest part.
Es la parte más larga.

3. The mouth of the uterus thins due to the contractions.
El cuello de la matriz enflaquece por las contracciones.

4. The contractions are light and irregular.
Las contracciones son ligeras e irregulares.

5. You may feel symptoms like menstrual cramps, diarrhea, back pain.
Se puede sentir síntomas como calambres menstruales, diarrea, dolor de espalda.

6. Engage in activities to keep your mind off the contractions.
Dedíquese a actividades que mantengan su mente alejada de las contracciones.

7. Take a warm shower.
Tome una ducha tibia.

8. If it is nighttime, try to sleep.
Si es de noche, trate de dormir.

9. Eat something light and drink plenty of fluids.
Coma algo liviano y tome muchos líquidos.

10. Take a walk in the fresh air.
Dé un paseo al aire fresco.

11. Relax and trust your body.
Relájese y confíe en su cuerpo.

12. Don´t rush off immediately to the hospital.
No salga corriendo al hospital

CHILDBIRTH EDUCATION
First Stage: Labor

Dilation
(*La Dilatación*)

1. The uterus contracts repeatedly to dilate and open the mouth of the uterus.
El útero se contrae repetidas veces para dilatar y abrir el cuello del útero.

2. The dilation is measured in centimeters, from 0-10.
La dilatación se mide en centímetros desde cero a diez.

3. Five to eight centimeters is active labor.
Cinco a ocho centímetros es el parto activo.

4. The contractions become more regular, prolonged, intense and frequent.
Las contracciones se hacen más regulares, prolongadas, intensas y frecuentes.

5. The baby continues to settle into the pelvis.
El bebé continúa acomodándose en la pelvis.

6. Try to relax in a comfortable position.
Trate de relajarse en una posición cómoda.

7. Rest between contractions.
Descanse entre contracciones.

8. Rest on your left side.
Descanse en su lado izquierdo.

9. Change positions frequently.
Cambie de posiciones frecuentemente.

10. Urinate every one to two hours.
Orine cada una a dos horas.

11. Use your controlled breathing and relaxation techniques.
Use las técnicas de respiración y relajación.

12. Listen carefully to the instructions of your coach.
Escuche cuidadosamente las instrucciones de su ayudante.

CHILDBIRTH EDUCATION
First Stage: Labor

Transition
(*La Transición*)

1. It is the period of eight to ten centimeters.
Es el periodo de ocho a diez centímetros.

2. It is the most difficult part of labor.
Es la parte más difícil del trabajo.

3. It is the shortest part.
Es la parte más breve.

4. The contractions may have multiple peaks.
Las contracciones pueden tener cimas múltiples.

5. It can seem one continuous contraction.
Puede parecer una contracción continua.

6. The contractions are at their maximum intensity.
Las contracciones están a su intensidad máxima.

7. You may feel the urge to push.
Es posible que sienta el deseo de pujar.

8. Tell your nurse when you feel the urge to push.
Dígale a su enfermera cuando siente la necesidad de pujar.

9. Keep your eyes open and concentrate on your focal point.
Mantenga los ojos abiertos y concéntrese en su punto focal.

10. Breathe in a way that helps you.
Respire de un modo que la alivie.

11. Follow your instincts.
Siga sus instintos.

12. Remember, this is the shortest stage of labor and will be over soon.
Recuerde que es la etapa más breve y pasará pronto.

CHILDBIRTH EDUCATION
Second Stage: Delivery

The Delivery
(El Parto)

1. The cervix is completely dilated.
La cerviz está completamente dilatada.

2. You will begin to push to birth the baby.
Empezará a pujar para expulsar al bebé.

3. The baby's head is presented (crowns).
Se presenta la cabeza del bebé (corona).

4. You will first birth the head and then the rest of the baby.
Se da a luz a la cabeza y luego al resto del bebé.

5. There is more time between contractions.
Hay más tiempo entre las contracciones.

6. You will feel the progression of the baby through the birth canal.
Sentirá el progreso del bebé por el canal del nacimiento.

7. You may feel a burning or stretching sensation.
Puede que sienta una sensación de ardor y estiramiento.

8. The pressure of the baby's head will be felt after each contraction.
La presión de la cabeza se puede sentir después de cada contracción

9. Push how and when your doctor tells you.
Puje como y cuando se lo indique su doctor.

10. The delivery can take from three minutes to two hours.
El parto puede llevar de tres minutos hasta dos horas.

11. It usually takes about forty minutes for the first baby.
Suele completarse en unos cuarenta minutos para el primer bebé.

12. It usually takes less time with subsequent births.
Suele completarse en menos tiempo para los siguientes partos.

CHILDBIRTH EDUCATION
Third Stage: Delivery of the Placenta

Delivery of the Placenta
(*El Nacimiento de la Placenta*)

1. It is hastened by breastfeeding the baby immediately after birth.
Es apresurado por el amamantamiento del bebé después del parto.

2. Hormones, either synthetic or natural, stimulate the contractions of the uterus.
Hormonas, sintéticas o naturales, estimulan las contracciones del útero.

3. It occurs five to twenty minutes after the birth.
Ocurre entre cinco a veinte minutos después del parto.

4. Normally with only one contraction the placenta is delivered
Normalmente con una sola contracción se expulsa la placenta.

CHILDBIRTH EDUCATION
Language Activities and Learning Strategies

Instructions: Set your own time frame for the following activities. It is recommended that a beginning learner allow three months for this unit, dedicating approximately 30 minutes a day to the goal of learning Spanish for prenatal care.

Unit 2 Begin Date: _____
Projected End Date: _____

A. Key Phrases

Listen to the phrases presented on pages 46-68 of the book on the audio program. These phrases will help you to communicate with a Spanish-speaking client about the common discomforts of pregnancy. You will also learn phrases that will help you to educate and inform your client about her pregnancy. Repeat each phrase out loud after the instructor in Spanish. Try to imitate the pronunciation as closely as you can. Listen for the vocabulary you already know. This will help you gain confidence as you recognize familiar structures. Repeat this exercise as often as needed to impress these structures on your memory. When you are confident of the pronunciation, select 90 phrases that you find most useful to you. Place each phrase on a separate index card. Memorize one phrase per day until you have learned all 90 phrases (1 phrase per day x 90 days = 3 months).

B. Targeted Grammar and Structure: Forming Commands

In order to communicate instructions appropriate to childbirth education, you need to be able to form commands in Spanish. In order to convey a message of respect, we are going to offer advice and communicate instructions using the formal you *(usted)* form. When you have become more familiar with your client, you may switch to the informal *(tú)* form. The grammar for constructing commands in the *usted* (formal you) form is simple. The rule is the following:

Rule:

Verbs in Spanish end in one of 3 ways: **ar, er, ir**.
Example: tom**ar** (to take), com**er** (to eat) and viv**ir** (to live).

To form commands using *usted* (formal you) there are three simple rules:

a. if a verb ends in **ar** (hablar) remove the **ar** and add **e** and you will have the command.
   Example: evit**ar** ---- evit ---- evit**e** (avoid)

b. if a verb ends in **er** (comer) remove the **er** & add **a**
   Example: com**er** ---- com ---- com**a** (eat)

c. if a verb ends in **ir** (vivir) remove the **ir** and add **a**
   Example: viv**ir** ---- viv ---- viv**a** (live)

Note: Above is the rule. There are always exceptions. In Spanish you will find many irregular commands. There is no way for you to know which verbs conjugate as irregular commands except through usage and by referring to a verb book for verification.

The following are 3 key commands that are useful when advising a patient about her pregnancy:

evite (ay.**bee**.tay): avoid
coma (**coe**.mah): eat
tome (**toe**.may): take

Learn these three commands and make them part of your working vocabulary. These three words are vital to communicating valuable advice on prenatal care.

C. Targeted Grammar and Structure: Questions

To form a question in Spanish, place the subject pronoun <u>after</u> the verb. Place an inverted question mark before the question and a question mark at the end of the sentence. Example:

<u>Usted</u> *tiene buen apetito.* (statement)
¿*Tiene* <u>usted</u> *buen apetito?* (question)

Question Words in Spanish

¿Quién? (Who?)
¿Qué? (What?)
¿Cuándo? (When?)
¿Dónde? (Where?)
¿Por qué? (Why?)
¿Cuánto? (How much? / How long?)
¿Cómo? (How?)
¿Cuál? (Which?)

D. Language Learning Activities

Answer the following questions using the foods listed on page 73.

a. ¿Qué comió ayer para el desayuno?

_____

b. ¿Qué comió ayer para el almuerzo?

_____

c. ¿Qué comió ayer para la cena?

_____

d. ¿Qué comió ayer para la merienda?

_____

e. ¿Cuál es tu comida favorita?

_____

Vocabulario Especializado: La Comida

Arroz: *rice*
Avena: *oatmeal*
Carne: *meat*
Carne de res: *beef*
Cereal: *cereal*
Ensalada: *salad*
Fruta: *fruit*
Habichuelas: *beans*
Huevo: *egg*
Jamón: *ham*
Jugo: *juice*
Leche: *milk*
Manzana: apple
Pan: *bread*
Pan tostado: *toast*
Panqueques: *pancakes*
Papa: *potato*
Papas Fritas: *French fries*
Pescado: *fish*
Pollo: *chicken*
Queso: *cheese*
Refresco: *soft drink*
Salchicha: *sausage*
Sandwich: *sandwich*
Sopa: *soup*
Tocino: *bacon*
Toronja: *grapefruit*
Viandas: *root vegetables*
Vegetales: *vegetables*

Cultural Reading
Nobody's Listening to Me !

A major question currently being posed by health professionals is why health messages seem to not reach, or are not heeded by, Spanish-speaking clientele. Researchers have not found the definitive answer to this question of non-compliance, but have discovered some common contributing factors. Many of these factors are rooted in the values and beliefs of the culture. Others are attributed to the limited educational level and an acute sense of powerlessness common among women of many Spanish-speaking communities now residing in the United States.

In traditional families, the Latina is not trained to question, to assert herself. She has been taught since childhood to leave all matters outside the home to the male authority figure, be it father, brother or eventually husband. Because of this lack of empowerment, you will see few Latin women from traditional cultures actively seeking out education in childbirth or complying with suggestions to improve her prenatal health and general well-being.

If we don't begin to intervene in a culturally-relevant manner, we will see an endless cycle of disempowerment and, subsequently, impoverished prenatal care.

Hopefully through education, first our own and then our clients', we will be able to break this cycle of powerlessness and help Latina woman from traditional cultures to experience a positive birth and then to relate that experience to the next generation.

Another thing you may have noticed is that the Latin mind functions best in the present, with immediate concerns taking precedence over those that may or may not take place in the future.

There is a somewhat fatalistic attitude shared by members of Spanish-speaking communities. The belief is that if something is going to happen, it will and there is nothing anyone can do to prevent it. Therefore why should one deprive oneself of enjoyable, if not necessarily healthy, foods and habits?

Time orientation tends to be in the present instead of the future. There is a sense of powerlessness about controlling the future, so planning and prevention are undervalued. It is God, not Man, who controls the future as well as any health outcome. Such a world view will obviously act as a deterrent to seeking preventive health care, or to heeding advice for a healthy pregnancy. Therefore, you should not be too surprised if the advice you offer goes unheeded, especially any advice you may give on diet, nutrition and good eating habits for a healthy pregnancy.

Respect for authority figures may cause Latinos to express agreement and understanding so as not to offend you, thus the seemingly compliant behavior. They see you as a health official, as one who should be given not only respect but also admiration.

Consequently, it may appear as if you have made great progress in your client's compliance only to find that your well-intended advice was never actually heeded.

There are also practical as well as cultural issues that interfere with compliance, such as lack of childcare, transportation, and time. Your Hispanic clients may not understand the American system of appointments, which is different from that in their own countries.

Most Latin American countries do not have such a structured system of medical appointments as that found in the United States. An "appointment" *(cita)* in many Spanish-speaking countries means a particular day, not a specific time, when a woman will be seen on a first come, first served basis. This may explain why your Hispanic client may arrive late for her scheduled appointment, not understanding the punctuality that is required of the American system.

Another important issue to keep in mind is that the concept of education as we know it does not exist in the lower-class Hispanic communities from where many of your Spanish-speaking patients originate. We think nothing of going to a class to further our knowledge. We have been going to classes all our lives.

For a migrant worker, who has three years at best of formal education and very little experience going to "school," attending a childbirth education class will not be seen as a priority.

After all, childbirth is considered a state of well-being in most Spanish-speaking countries. Education about pregnancy doesn't make a whole lot of sense for a woman who will learn most of what she has to learn about her pregnancy from her mother or other female family members.

Just as education is not given a high value in lower income Spanish-speaking communities, nor has exercise achieved much importance in the every-day life of Hispanic women. To affect positive change in this area, think more on a group rather than individual level. As much as a Latin woman may wish to exercise, she will most likely not do so alone. Encourage group exercise and offer alternatives to individualized activities.

Encourage changes in diet on a group level as well. Diet is an integral part of a person's culture, and ethnicity will have a profound effect on nutrition.

Traditional foods are very important to ethnic groups and define their diet. Puerto Ricans, for example, rarely eat green or leafy vegetables and only occasionally use milk and eggs. Starchy vegetables, such as the potato (*papa*), pumpkin (*calabaza*), *yucca*, green banana (*plátano*), sweet potato (*batata*), and other tubers like *yautía* and *ñame* are often boiled in stews. The *plátano* is an especially versatile vegetable. Fried, crushed and refried it makes *tostones* or *arañitas*. To this starchy diet, Puerto Ricans add fats in liberal quantities. Fried foods are popular and meat (mostly pork) is cooked in generous portions of oil or lard. Beans and meat are the main sources of protein, and rice and beans is a staple on the island.

When counseling on diet and nutrition, you need to be aware of individual eating preferences and be able to help your clients to make the most of their ethnic diets. For example, to tell a Mexican-American to eat peanut butter or cottage cheese is counter-productive. To tell her to prepare more chicken with the family's rice and beans, however, might probably meet with success.

Besides making the most of ethnic diets, make the most of the father's participation in his partner's care. Appeal to his natural tendency to want to protect his wife. Say to him, *El embarazo de su mujer puede ser sana y segura si anima a su esposa a que coma mejor.* (Your wife's pregnancy can be healthier and safer if you encourage her to eat better). *Ella necesita comer una variedad de alimentos que sean saludables para ella.* (She needs to eat a variety of foods that are healthy for her). As you proceed to tell him about the benefits and nature of good nutrition, add the following, critical piece of advice: *Cuídese usted también. Si usted come comidas nutritivas, le ayudará a ella a que haga lo mismo.* (Take care of yourself as well. If you eat nutritious foods, this will help her to do the same).

Always keep in mind that your Hispanic clients will most likely not be successful on an individual level. If changes are to be made, they are to be made on a group or family level. The father can be critical to the success or failure of a new health plan. He can encourage his wife to make the necessary changes. His position of authority and respect in the family can be a powerful catalyst to change.

Work with him, or with other significant family members, before you try to counsel the mom. She will be more influenced by what significant family members say and do than by what the health care provider advises. Family members can have a substantial influence on what decisions are made. Their power to influence decisions should be used to your advantage when imparting messages concerning diet and nutrition. When you impart those messages, however, remember that a structured, instructive approach is usually expected and responded to most favorably within the Hispanic community.

Questions for Discussion

1. What cultural factors and beliefs contribute to non-compliant behavior and how can you work towards changing non-compliant behavior into compliance?

2. What practical obstacles are presented as barriers to receiving adequate prenatal care and education within the Hispanic community?

3. What impact does ethnicity have on prenatal nutrition and how can you help make the most of ethnic diets when teaching about healthy eating habits for pregnancy?

4. What is the most successful strategy for implementing change in diet and eating habits?

Unit Three
AT THE BIRTH CENTER

Admissions
Initial Preparation and Orientation
Labor and Delivery
Medications in Labor
Cesarean Delivery
Reaching Out to the Father
Key Question Words in Spanish
Informing with "Le voy a . . ."
Key Commands for Labor and Delivery
Communicating with the Laboring Mom

AT THE BIRTH CENTER
Admissions

1. Do you have contractions?
¿Tiene contracciones?

2. What time did the contractions begin?
¿A qué hora le empezaron las contracciones?

3. How long does each contraction last?
¿Cuánto le dura cada contracción?

4. How far apart are the contractions?
¿Con qué frecuencia tiene las contracciones?

5. Have the membranes ruptured? When?
¿Rompió fuente? ¿Cuándo?

6. What color was the fluid? Clear? Yellow? Green?
¿Qué color tenía el líquido? ¿Claro? ¿Amarillo? ¿Verde?

7. Are you bleeding?
¿Está sangrando?

8. How much? A cupful? A tablespoon? A teaspoon?
¿Cuánto? ¿Una taza? ¿Una cucharada? ¿Una cucharadita?

9. When is your due date?
¿Cuándo es su fecha de parto? (en Puerto Rico) ¿Cuándo se alivia? (en México)

10. Who is your doctor? Pediatrician?
¿Quién es su doctor? ¿Pediatra?

11. Have you contacted him?
¿Le ha notificado?

12. Who is accompanying you? What is his relationship to you?
¿Quién le acompaña? ¿Cuál es su parentesco?

13. We are not going to admit you now.
No la vamos a ingresar ahora.

14. You are not in labor.
Usted no está de parto.

15. You are in early labor.
Usted está de parto temprano.

16. Go home and rest.
Regrese a casa y descanse.

17. Come back when the contractions are stronger and every five to ten minutes.
Regrese cuando las contracciones estén más fuertes y cada cinco a diez minutos.

18. Come back if your bag of water breaks.
Regrese si rompa fuente.

19. Have you had any problems with this pregnancy?
¿Ha tenido algún problema con este embarazo?

20. Have you had any infections?
¿Ha tenido alguna infección?

21. Have you had swelling?
¿Ha tenido hinchazón?

22. Have you had blurred vision?
¿Ha tenido la visión borrosa?

23. Have you had severe headaches?
¿Ha tenido dolores fuertes de cabeza?

24. Have you had difficulty breathing?
¿Ha tenido dificultad para respirar?

25. Have you had heart palpitations?
¿Ha tenido palpitaciones del corazón?

26. Have you had abdominal pain?
¿Ha tenido dolor abdominal?

27. Have you had constipation/diarrhea?
¿Ha tenido estreñimiento/diarrea?

28. Have you had nausea or vomiting?
¿Ha tenido náusea o vómitos?

29. Have you had difficulty urinating?
¿Ha tenido dificultad para orinar?

30. Have you moved your bowels?
¿Ha evacuado?

31. What is your present weight?
¿Cuál es su peso actual?

32. How much weight did you gain during your pregnancy?
¿Cuántas libras ha aumentado durante el embarazo?

33. How tall are you?
¿Cuánto mide?

34. Are you taking any medications?
¿Está tomando algún medicamento?

35. Are you allergic to penicillin or other antibiotics?
¿Es alérgica a la penicilina u otros antibióticos?

36. Are you allergic to morphine, codeine, or other narcotics?
¿Es alérgica a la morfina, codeína u otros narcóticos?

37. Are you allergic to Novocain or other anesthetics?
¿Es alérgica a la novocaína u otros tipos de anestesia?

38. Are you allergic to iodine or other antiseptics?
¿Es alérgica al yodo u otros antisépticos?

39. Are you allergic to latex?
¿Es alérgica al latex?

40. What is your religion?
¿Cuál es su religión?

41. Does this hospitalization create any economic, family, or emotional problems for you?
¿Le crea esta hospitalización algún problema económico, familiar, o emocional?

42. Please sign this consent form.
Por favor, firme esta forma de consentimiento.

AT THE BIRTH CENTER
Initial Preparation and Orientation

1. I need a urine sample.
Necesito una muestra de orina.

2. Go to the bathroom.
Vaya al baño.

3. Put on this gown.
Póngase esta bata.

4. Lie down.
Acuéstese.

5. Get comfortable.
Póngase cómoda.

6. I am going to take your blood pressure.
Le voy a tomar la presión sanguínea.

7. I am going to take your temperature.
Le voy a tomar la temperatura.

8. I am going to take a blood sample.
Le voy a tomar una muestra de sangre.

9. I am going to prick you.
Le voy a pinchar.

10. Breathe deeply.
Respire profundo.

11. I am going to start an I.V.
Le voy a poner un suero.

12. It will give you fluids.
Le dará líquidos.

13. I am going to administer an enema.
Le voy a administrar un enema.

14. It will not hurt.
No le va a molestar.

15. I am going to shave you.
Le voy a rasurar (en Puerto Rico) afeitar (en México).

16. I am going to connect you to a fetal monitor.
Le voy a conectar a un monitor fetal.

17. It allows us to listen to the baby's heartbeat.
Esto nos permite escuchar el latido del corazón del bebé.

18. It also measures the intensity of your contractions.
Esto mide también la intensidad de sus contracciones.

19. I am going to insert this wire.
Le voy a poner este alambrecito.

20. It attaches to the baby´s head.
Se pega a la cabeza del bebé.

21. It allows us to hear the baby´s heartbeat better.
Nos ayuda a escuchar mejor los latidos del corazón del bebé.

22. I am going to examine you to see if you have begun to dilate.
Le voy a examinar para ver si ha empezado a dilatar.

23. Relax.
Relájese.

24. You have dilated five centimeters.
Ha dilatado hasta cinco centímetros.

25. I am going to ask you some questions to complete your medical record.
Le voy a hacer unas preguntas para completar su historial médico.

AT THE BIRTH CENTER
Labor and Delivery

1. Relax.
Relájese.

2. Breathe deeply.
Respire profundo.

3. Breathe slowly and evenly.
Respire lento e igualmente.

4. Breathe when the contraction begins.
Respire al empezar la contracción.

5. Inhale through the nose.
Inhale por la nariz.

6. Exhale through the mouth.
Exhale por la boca.

7. Calm down.
Tranquilícese.

8. Breathe with me.
Respire conmigo.

9. Close your eyes.
Cierre los ojos.

10. Think about your baby and how much you love him.
Piense en su bebé y en cuánto lo ama.

11. Allow your body to open up for your baby.
Permita que el cuerpo ceda y se abra para su bebé.

12. Take control
Tome el control.

13. Concentrate on a focal point.
Concéntrese en un punto focal.

14. Do you want to change position?
¿Desea cambiar de posición?

15. Do you need to use the bathroom?
¿Necesita usar el baño?

16. Do you want to walk?
¿Desea caminar?

17. The labor will progress more rapidly.
El parto progresará más rápido.

18. You are eight centimeters dilated.
Está dilatada hasta ocho centímetros.

19. Don't give up.
No se rinda.

20. Trust me.
Confíe en mí.

21. Trust your body .
Confíe en su cuerpo.

22. Blow when you feel the urge to push.
Sople cuando sienta el impulso de pujar.

23. Rest for a moment.
Descanse un ratito.

24. You are fully dilated.
Está completamente dilatada.

25. You are going to push now to birth the baby.
Va a pujar ahora para expulsar al bebé.

26. Push.
Puje.

27. Push again.
Puje otra vez.

28. Harder. Keep going.
Con más fuerza. Sígalo.

29. Grab your knees and push.
Agarre las rodillas y puje.

30. Hold your breath and push.
Aguante la respiración y puje.

31. Put your chin on your chest and push.
Ponga la barbilla (México) la chiva (Puerto Rico) al pecho.

32. Push and hold onto it.
Puje y no lo corte.

33. Bear down.
Puje abajo.

34. Push as if you were having a bowel movement.
Puje como si fuera a evacuar.

35. The head is presenting (crowning).
La cabeza se está presentando (coronando).

36. Don´t push.
No puje.

37. Congratulations!
¡Felicidades!

38. It's a boy.
Es un niño.

39. It's a girl.
Es una niña.

40. She is precious.
Ella es preciosa.

41. He is healthy and strong.
Él es sano y fuerte.

42. God bless him.
Dios lo bendiga.

43. God bless her.
Dios la bendiga.

AT THE BIRTH CENTER
Medications in Labor

1. We need to induce labor.
Tenemos que inducirle el trabajo de parto.

2. Labor is induced by inserting a small tablet into the cervix to stimulate dilation and ripening.
Se induce el trabajo de parto al insertar una pastillita en la cérviz para estimular la dilatación.

3. Would you like a sedative?
¿Le gustaría un sedante?

4. Would you like some medication to soothe the pain?
¿Desea algún medicamento para calmar el dolor?

5. Demerol is an analgesic that will help you relax and rest between contractions.
El Demerol es un analgésico que le ayudará a relajarse y a descansar entre contracciones.

6. The effects of this drug are relatively short, between thirty minutes to three hours.
Los efectos de esta droga son relativamente cortos, entre treinta minutos y tres horas.

7. This drug is administered through the I.V. or an intramuscular injection.
Se administra este medicamento mediante el suero o una inyección intramuscular.

8. The epidural is a stronger method of pain relief.
El epidural es un método más eficaz para aliviar el dolor.

9. The lower part of your body will be completely numb.
La parte baja del cuerpo estará completamente adormecida.

10. The effects of this drug can last up to ten hours.
Los efectos de este medicamento pueden durar hasta diez horas.

11. This drug is administered through a catheter in the epidural space.
Se administra este medicamento mediante un catéter en el espacio epidural.

12. We need to stimulate your contractions to help labor progress.
Necesitamos estimular las contracciones para que progrese el parto.

13. I am going to give you pitocin to make your contractions stronger.
Le voy a dar pitocina para hacerle más fuertes las contracciones.

AT THE BIRTH CENTER
Cesarean Delivery

1. There are complications.
Hay complicacciones.

2. The baby is too big for your pelvis.
El bebé es demasiado grande para su pelvis.

3. The baby is not receiving enough oxygen.
El bebé no está recibiendo suficiente oxígeno.

4. Your blood pressure is very high.
Su presión está muy alta.

5. The cord is wrapped around the baby's neck.
El cordón está enredado al cuello del bebé.

6. The baby is in breech/transverse position.
El bebé viene de nalgas (transverso).

7. The placenta has separated from the uterus.
La placenta se ha separado del útero.

8. We have to do an emergency cesarean.
Tenemos que hacerle una cesárea de emergencia.

9. We are going now to the operating room.
Nos vamos ya a la Sala de Operaciones.

10. I am going to take your vital signs.
Le voy a tomar sus signos vitales.

11. I am going to connect you to an electrocardiogram.
Le voy a conectar a un electrocardiograma.

12. I am going to shave and disinfect the area of the operation.
Le voy a afeitar y desinfectar el área de la operación.

13. I am putting in a catheter so that the bladder does not swell during surgery.
Estoy poniendo un catéter para que la vejiga no se hinche durante la cirugía.

14. The anesthesiologist will administer a medication that will numb you from the waist down.
El anestesiólogo le administrará un medicamento que le adormecerá desde la cintura para abajo.

15. Don´t worry.
No se preocupe.

16. Everything will be fine.
Todo estará bien.

17. I will be here with you.
Estaré aquí con usted.

18. I will explain what the doctor is doing.
Le explicaré lo que está haciendo el doctor.

19. The doctor is making an incision into your skin.
El doctor está haciendo una incisión en la piel.

20. Now he is opening the uterus.
Ahora está abriendo el útero.

21. He is taking out your baby.
Está sacando a su bebé.

22. Now he is clamping and cutting the cord.
Ahora está pinchando y cortando el cordón.

23. He is removing the placenta.
Está sacando la placenta.

24. He is closing up the two incisions with staples / stiches.
Está cerrando las dos incisiones con grapas / puntos.

AT THE BIRTH CENTER
Reaching Out to the Father

1. Sit with her.
Siéntate con ella.

2. Give her a massage.
Dale un masaje.

3. Caress her hair.
Acaricia su pelo.

4. Put on meditation music for her.
Ponla música de meditación.

5. Hug her.
Abrázala.

6. Breathe with her.
Respira con ella.

7. Don't leave her alone.
No la dejes sola.

8. Give her some ice chips.
Dale pedacitos de hielo.

9. Moisten her lips.
Humedézcale los labios.

10. Change her position.
Cámbiala de posición.

11. Kiss her.
Bésala.

12. Take her hand.
Tómala de la mano.

13. Give her caring and love.
Dále cariño y amor.

AT THE BIRTH CENTER
Language Activities and Learning Strategies

Instructions: Set your own time frame for the following activities. It is recommended that a beginning learner allow three months for this unit, dedicating approximately 30 minutes a day to the goal of learning Spanish for prenatal care.

Unit 3: Begin Date: _____
Projected End Date: _____

A. Key Phrases

Listen to the phrases presented on pages 81-101 of the book on the audio program. These phrases will help you to communicate with a Spanish-speaking client in a birth setting, from admissions to delivery. Repeat each phrase out loud after the instructor in Spanish. Try to imitate the pronunciation as closely as you can. Listen for the vocabulary you already know. This will help you gain confidence as you recognize familiar structures. Repeat this exercise as often as needed to learn the vocabulary and terminology presented. When you are confident of the pronunciation, select 90 phrases that you find most useful to you. Place each phrase on a separate index card. Memorize one phrase per day until you have learned all 90 phrases.

B. Targeted Grammar and Structure: Forming Questions with Key Verbs

In order to obtain information to be able to complete patient admissions forms and to inquire about patient needs during labor and delivery, you will need to be able to ask questions in Spanish. There are four key question words in Spanish that will allow you to ask the right questions and receive the answers you are looking for. They are as follows:

tiene: (tee.**yen**.eh): Do you have?
ha tenido: (ah.ten.**ee**.though): Have you had?
desea: (day.**say**.ah): Do you want?
necesita: (nay.say.**see**.tah): Do you need?

Practice these 4 question words several times, following the phonetic guide provided above. Learn these words and make them a part of your working vocabulary. These 4 words will allow you to ask questions in Spanish in many areas of perinatal care.

C. Targeted Grammar and Structure: Informing with le voy a . . .

Part of your job as a nurse is to inform your patient about treatments and procedures. The proper way to inform a patient in Spanish is to use the following structure:

Le voy a + Infinitive (I am going to . . .)

Example: *Le voy a examinar.*
(I am going to examine you).

Complete the following sentences using the correct infinitive. Refer to pages 87 to 89 of your workbook for help with this exercise.

Le voy a _____
(take your blood pressure).

Le voy a _____
(take your temperature).

Le voy a _____
(take a blood sample).

Le voy a _____
(start an IV line).

Le voy a _____
(connect you to a fetal monitor).

Le voy a _____
(examinar).

D. Targeted Grammar and Structure: Key Commands

In this section you have learned how to guide a Spanish-speaking patient through her labor and delivery using relaxation and breathing techniques. You will need to use commands to successfully complete this function. One strategy for assimilating the Spanish of childbirth is to study by focusing on key verbs. The following are 9 key commands (verb forms) you will need to communicate instructions during labor and delivery:

Key Verbs

relájese: (ray.**lah**.hay.say): relax
respire: (res.**peer**.ray): breathe
inhale: (in.**ah**.lay): inhale
exhale: (x.**ah**.lay): exhale
tranquilícese: (trahn.key.**lee**.say.say): relax
concéntrese: (cone.**sen**.tray.say): concentrate
sople: (sow.play): blow
descanse: (des.**kahn**.say): rest
puje: (**poo**.hay): push

Practice these commands several times, following the phonetic pronunciation guide provided above. Learn these 9 commands and make them a part of your working vocabulary for labor and delivery. Then listen to the commands presented on pages 90-94 of your text on the audio program. Repeat each phrase out loud in Spanish after the instructor. Try to imitate the pronunciation as closely as you can. Listen for the commands outlined above. Repeat this exercise many times until you feel comfortable with the material.

E. Language Learning Activities

Select 20 of the commands presented on pages 90-94 which you use most frequently on your job. Mark them in your text. Practice the phrases orally several times until you are confident of the pronunciation and the words flow smoothly. Read the selected commands into your recorder. Replay your recording and listen for any errors in pronunciation.

Cultural Reading
Communicating With Laboring Moms: Culturally and Linguistically

Hispanic women often come to give birth in U.S. hospitals with a great deal of fear and misinformation, for many reasons. First of all, she may be alone. Her husband may have left her in the emergency room, to give birth to her child without him. He is not usually doing this out of lack of compassion or concern, but more likely because he was not given leave from work and fears losing his job, or because he fears that by admitting her to the hospital, he is inviting immigration to deport them both from the country. This woman, left to birth her baby alone, probably does not speak the language nor does she understand the complex biomedical culture to which she is suddenly exposed.

Or, you may have the opposite problem: the entire family at the bedside ready and willing to give help and advice. Loyalty to family is a cherished value within the Latino culture. Therefore, when one family member is hospitalized, you will most likely have not only the patient to attend, but the spouse (often very uncomfortable with his role as a caregiver), the mother, grandmother and any other member of the family who happens to be in the area at the time.

The importance and the challenges of group support should be recognized on many levels when working with Spanish-speaking communities.

One challenge of this family dynamic is that female family members often inadvertently pass on the misinformation and cultural myths that they internalized with the birth of their own children. Lacking adequate prenatal preparation, some women have internalized the belief that birth is a dangerous, painful event that will cause her pain and suffering. Perhaps she has seen her mother agonize over a difficult birth at home, or has heard the stories of a sibling who died at birth.

These fears are often handed down from generation to generation and eventually are accepted as basic truths. Coupled with lack of information, an acute sense of powerlessness, and a frightening language barrier, the Latina often comes to birth her own baby with doubt, insecurity, and a great deal of fear and misinformation. What is difficult for us to understand in all this is not the fear or the pain, but the Latina expression of it.

You may hear some Latin women moaning *ay-ay-ay* during contractions, letting their emotion carry the rhythm louder, higher, and faster as labor progresses. This type of release tends to conflict with the approach of health providers from the American culture who value stoicism and limited, non-emotional expressions of pain.

Some American childbirth professionals feel that their job is well done if the floor is quiet. Silence means that everything is orderly, in control, and that the patients are comfortable and progressing efficiently. For many Latinos, however, not expressing emotion during occasions of pain or suffering would seem unnatural.

The Latino, men and women alike, is very expressive in all emotions ranging from joy to pain, grief and fear. You may have heard expressions such as ¡*Diós Mío! ¡No puedo!* (Oh my God, I can´t). ¡*No puedo más!* (I can´t do it anymore). ¡*Me muero!* (I´m dying). ¡*No aguanto más!* (I can´t bear it anymore). Such expressions, accompanied by an outburst of emotion, are common socio-linguistic characteristics of some Latino cultures. How do you respond to the emotional needs of your laboring Latina moms in a culturally-responsible way?

Many nurses enter into a state of cultural shock when they first encounter emotions with which they are uncomfortable. Often the first reaction to such a shock is to either retreat, or to go for the pain medication.

The truth is that your Spanish-speaking patient probably does not expect any medication, nor does she necessarily want it. She does not receive it routinely in her own country. Medications are expensive and not readily available. Epidurals are used only in cesarean deliveries, and are therefore feared, the association being that if an epidural is administered, there must be a complication that is leading to a cesarean.

Her culture has simply taught her that pain is expressed. Do not be intimidated or fearful of the emotions you will become a part of. Emotion is a normal reaction to pain in the Latin culture. Learn to work with your Spanish-speaking patient, helping her to temper her emotions in a positive way.

Touch will prove a vital force in soothing and calming a patient who appears out of control. Latinos are very demonstrative. They enjoy touching and receiving warmth from others through touch. Touch your patient and soothe her with some gentle words of compassion, words like *No se preocupe* (Don't worry). *Todo va bién.* (Everything is fine). *Estoy contigo.* I am with you). *Le ayudaré.* (I will help you).

When she says, ¡*No puedo!* ¡*No aguanto más!* (I can´t. I can´t bear it anymore). You say, *Sí puede. Lo está haciendo.* (Yes you can. You are doing it). When she says, ¡*Ah, ah, ah. Me muero!* (I´m dying). You say, *No se muere.* (You´re not dying). *Yo sé que tiene mucho dolor.* (I know that you are in a lot of pain). *El dolor ayuda a que nazca su bebé.* (The pain is helping your baby to be born). *Es normal.* (It's normal). What you are doing is empowering your client to take more control of her pain, while at the same time empathizing with her suffering.

Even more challenging than dealing with a type of pain expression foreign to our own is the situation which often presents itself when the mother or a female companion of the laboring mom offers conflicting advice to her daughter at important transitions throughout the progress of labor.

It is very important when this occurs to re-direct your patient's care to yourself, without offending the family member. Touch the mother lightly on the hand and assure her that you have things under control. That physical contact will do two things: 1) make her feel more comfortable with you, and consequently 2) encourage her to concede control of the progress of labor over to you.

Kindly, but firmly you should assure her that you will do what is best for her daughter. You may say something like: *No se preocupe, señora. Todo va bién. Déjeme ayudar a su hija.* (Don't worry, Madam. Everything is going well. Let me help your daughter).

When she feels confident that you are there to help her daughter, you will see a change of attitude and a smoother bedside-care situation. Remember, you are seen as an authority and a person demanding of respect. If you gain the confidence of the family members of the woman you are assisting, you will also gain their respect and cooperation.

Even despite the conflicts that may occur with female family members accompanying a birthing mom, they do not pose the same challenge as the male companions or spouses present for the delivery of their child.

Hispanic society has traditionally given the male a paternalistic role and a position of authority in most matters outside of the home. As a decision-maker he functions well. Put him in the role of caregiver, however, and he is often uncomfortable.

The role of nurturer and healer has always been that of the female family members. You may have to coax a male support person out of his macho role and help him soothe his nervous wife.

Offer him suggestions on how he can participate in this foreign role, suggestions like *Séquele la frente*. (Wipe her brow). *Sostenga la mano*. (Hold her hand). *Sóbele la espalda*. (Rub her back). B*reathe with her*. (Respire con ella). *Siéntese con ella*. (Sit with her) or *No la deje sóla*. (Don't leave her alone). With these words you are empowering the father to participate in a role he is most likely uncomfortable with while at the same time allowing him to sooth and calm his anxious wife.

After guiding his support, reassure him that his presence is valued and appreciated by both you and his wife. Say, *Su contacto y palabras amables le significan mucho a ella* (Your contact and friendly words mean a lot to her). You may also offer him words of encouragement like, *Su esposa está bién*. (Your wife is fine). *Necesita descansar un ratito*. (She just needs to rest for a while). *Porque no descansa usted mismo*. (Why don't you take some rest yourself). This type of encouragement will put the nervous husband at ease and better help him to support his laboring wife.

You can work effectively with members of culturally-diverse families if you demonstrate understanding and gain the confidence of family members. You will eventually find the group support comforting and helpful as you learn to direct it appropriately.

Questions for Discussion

1. What challenges can family members pose to health-care providers helping a laboring mom?

2. What types of cultural myths and beliefs have some Latina woman internalized through life experience?

3. How have you seen pain expressed in the Latino culture? How do those expressions make you feel?

4. What are some strategies for dealing with pain expression that are foreign to your own?

Unit Four
MOTHER/INFANT CARE AND POSTPARTUM RECOVERY

Initial Recovery and Newborn Assessment
Discharge Instructions
The Benefits of Breastfeeding
Nursing Your Baby
Suggestions for Successful Breastfeeding
Alleviating Common Breast Discomforts
The Verb *Desea* and Postpartum Care
Forming Commands for Hospital Discharge
Forming Commands for Breastfeeding
Postpartum Myths and Taboos

MOTHER / INFANT CARE AND POSTPARTUM RECOVERY
Initial Recovery and Newborn Assessment

1. Your baby weighs six pounds 12 ounces.
Su bebé pesa seis libras con doce onzas.

2. He / she is eighteen inches long.
El / ella mide dieciocho pulgadas.

3. He / she is healthy and strong.
El / ella es sano/a y fuerte.

4. I am putting some drops into your baby´s eyes to prevent infection.
Estoy poniendo gotitas en los ojos de su bebé para prevenir una infección.

5. I am giving your baby an injection of vitamin K to help coagulate his blood.
Estoy administrando vitamina K para ayudar en la coagulación de la sangre.

6. I´m going to take a blood sample from your baby´s heel.
Voy a sacar una muestra de sangre del talón de su bebé.

7. This test will tell us if the baby has jaundice or low blood-sugar.
Esta prueba nos dirá si el bebé tiene ictericia o un bajo nivel de azúcar en la sangre.

8. It will only be a small prick.
Es un pinchazo, nada más.

9. Would you like me to put the baby on your chest?
¿Desea que ponga el bebé encima de su pecho?

10. Would you like to hold your baby?
¿Desea coger (en Puerto Rico) cargar (en México) a su bebé?

11. May I hold your baby?
¿Puedo cogerlo / la? (en Puerto Rico) ¿Puedo cargarlo / la? (en México)

12. Would you like to nurse your baby?
¿Desea lactar (en Puerto Rico) dar pecho (en México) a su bebé?

13. Do you want your baby to stay in the room with you?
¿Desea que su bebé se quede en el cuarto con usted?

14. Do you want the nurses to care for your baby in the nursery?
¿Desea que las enfermeras cuiden a su bebé en La Sala de Recién Nacidos?

15. When your baby is with you, always keep him covered so he does not catch cold.
Cuando su bebé esté con usted, manténgalo siempre cubierto para que no le de frío.

16. Lay your baby on his side or on his back.
Acueste a su bebé de lado o boca arriba.

17. Do not lay him on his stomach.
No lo acueste boca abajo.

18. Do you have cramps?
¿Tiene calambres?

19. The uterus is contracting as it returns to its normal size.
El útero está contrayéndose mientras regresa a su tamaño normal.

20. Massage your stomach to help the uterus contract.
Pase la mano sobre la barriga para ayudar a que el útero se contraiga.

21. Do you want a blanket?
¿Desea una frisa (en Puerto Rico) cobija (en México)?

22. Would you like to eat or drink something? Juice? Water? Tea?
¿Desea tomar algo? ¿Jugo? ¿Agua? ¿Té?

23. Would you like to take something for the pain?
¿Desea tomar algo para el dolor?

24. Would you like to take a shower?
¿Desea ducharse? (en México) ¿Bañarse? (en Puerto Rico)

25. Would you like a sitz bath?
¿Desea tomar un baño de asiento?

26. Would you like an ice pack?
¿Desea una bolsa de hielo?

27. Call the nurse for help the first time you get up.
Llame a la enfermera por ayuda la primera vez que se levante.

MOTHER / INFANT CARE AND POSTPARTUM RECOVERY
Discharge Instructions

I. PHYSICAL ACTIVITIES & EXERCISE
(*Actividades Físicas y Ejercicio*)

1. Walk without restriction.
Camine sin restricciones.

2. Begin gradually to return to a regular program of exercise.
Comience gradualmente a volver a hacer un programa de ejercicios.

3. Do mild exercises.
Haga ejercicios suaves.

4. Do Kegel exercises.
Haga los ejercicios Kegel.

5. Do not lift heavy objects (over ten pounds).
No levante objetos pesados (de más de diez libras).

6. Get a lot of rest.
Descanse mucho.

7. Rest as often as possible.
Descanse tanto como sea posible.

8. Rest when your baby sleeps.
Descanse cuando su bebé duerma.

9. Limit your activities to caring for your baby and yourself.
Limite sus actividades para el cuidado del bebé y de sí misma.

II. DIET & NUTRITION
(Alimentación y Dieta)

1. Continue to eat the same foods as recommended during pregnancy.
Siga comiendo los mismos alimentos que le recomendaron durante el embarazo.

2. If you are breastfeeding your baby, you should increase calorie intake by 300.
Aumenta la ingestión de calorías en 300 si lacta a su bebé.

3. Drink half a liter of milk daily.
Tome medio litro de leche diario.

4. Drink six to eight glasses of water daily.
Tome de seis a ocho vasos de agua diario.

5. Do not go on a diet when you are breastfeeding.
No se ponga a dieta cuando está lactando.

6. Continue taking prenatal vitamins.
Siga tomando vitaminas prenatales.

7. Continue taking a multivitamin daily.
Siga tomando multivitaminas diariamente.

8. It will not make you fat.
Esto no hará que aumente de peso.

III. VAGINAL BLEEDING
(Sangrado Vaginal)

1. You will have moderate amounts of vaginal bleeding.
Usted tendrá cantidades moderadas de sangrado vaginal.

2. It may last from four to six weeks.
Puede durar de cuatro a seis semanas.

3. Color may vary throughout the six-week period.
El color puede variar durante un periodo de seis semanas.

4. The blood will have an intense red color during the first 3 to 4 days postpartum.
La sangre tendrá un color rojo intenso durante los primeros 3 a 4 días después.

5. Then it will change to a rose color during the 4th to 14th day postpartum.
Luego cambiará a un color rosado durante el 4to a 14to día postparto.

6. Then it will change to a brown color during weeks two to six postpartum.
Luego cambiará a un color marrón durante las semanas dos a seis posparto.

7. It may contain blood clots.
Puede que contenga coágulos.

8. The blood should not have an offensive odor nor remnants of tissue.
El sangrado no debe tener mal olor ni tejido.

9. Use a sanitary pad instead of a tampon.
Use una toalla sanitaria en vez de un tampón.

10. Change your pad often.
Cambie la toalla sanitaria frecuentemente.

11. Do not use vaginal douches.
No use duchas vaginales.

12. Any foreign object inside the vagina may cause infection.
Cualquier material ajeno dentro de la vagina puede causar infección.

IV. THE EPISIOTOMY
(*La Episiotomía*)

1. You may experience some discomfort as the episiotomy heals.
Es posible que sienta algún malestar mientras sana la episiotomía.

2. The stiches will dissolve by themselves.
Los puntos se disolverán solos.

3. When you go to the bathroom, always wipe from front to back.
Cuando vaya al baño, séquese siempre de adelante hacia atrás.

4. Sit in a warm tub to relieve discomfort.
Siéntese en una bañera con agua tibia para aliviarse.

5. Apply a local anesthetic cream or spray to your sanitary napkin.
Aplique una crema anestética o un rociador medicado a su toalla sanitaria.

6. Sit on a soft pillow the first few days postpartum.
Siéntese sobre una almohadilla blanda durante los primeros días postparto.

7. After urinating, squirt warm water on your perineum with the peri-bottle we gave you.
Después de orinar, vierta un poco de agua tibia sobre el perineo con la botella que le dimos.

V. AFTER A CESAREAN
(Después de la Cesárea)

1. Get up and walk as soon as you can do so comfortably.
Levántese y camine lo más pronto posible sin fatigarse.

2. To relieve gas pains, breathe deeply and then exhale. Repeat several times.
Para aliviar el dolor de gases, respire profundo y luego exhale. Repita varias veces.

3. Avoid spicy or gas-causing foods.
Evite los alimentos condimentados que produzcan gas.

4. Avoid driving for the first few weeks postpartum.
Evite manejar las primeras semanas postparto.

5. Do not climb stairs or lift heavy objects.
No suba por escaleras. No levante objetos pesados.

6. Wash the incision with soap and water.
Lave la incisión con agua y jabón.

7. Air dry your wound after bathing.
Séquese la herida al aire después de bañarse.

VI. BREAST CARE
(Cuidado de los Senos)

1. Always wear a supportive cotton bra.
Use un sostén de algodón ajustado siempre.

2. Wash your breasts with soap and water.
Lave los senos con agua y jabón.

3. Do not use soap on the nipple.
No use jabón en el área del pezón.

4. Leave your nipples exposed to air until they are dry.
Deje los pezones expuestos al aire hasta que se sequen.

5. Massage your breasts to keep the milk ducts open.
Dele masaje a los senos para mantener los ductos de leche abiertos.

6. Put warm compresses on the breasts to relieve swelling.
Ponga compresas tibias sobre los senos para aliviar la hinchazón.

VII. MENSTRUACTION AND SEXUAL RELATIONS
(Menstruación y Relaciones Sexuales)

1. The menstrual cycle generally resumes in six to eight weeks.
El flujo menstrual generalmente regresa dentro de seis a ocho semanas.

2. It may take a little longer for women who are breastfeeding.
Puede tardar más en mujeres que lactan (en Puerto Rico) dan pecho (en México).

3. Your first two or three periods may be heavy, prolonged or irregular.
Sus primeras dos o tres menstruaciones pueden ser pesadas, prolongadas o irregulares.

4. It is possible to become pregnant even before you menstruate.
Es posible quedar embarazada antes de que regrese la menstruación.

5. It is possible to become pregnant while you are breastfeeding.
Es posible quedar embarazada mientras lacta.

6. Avoid having sexual relations for six weeks after the delivery.
Evite las relaciones sexuales por seis semanas después del parto.

7. If you used a diaphragm before, have it refitted after delivery.
Si usaba antes el diafragma, pida que la midan de nuevo después del parto.

8. If you are breastfeeding, do not take oral contraceptives without consulting with your doctor.
Si está lactando, no use anticonceptivos orales sin consultar a su doctor.

VIII. EMOTIONAL STATE
(Estado Emocional)

1. You may experience postpartum depression, anxiety, or crying without apparent cause.
Puede experimentar depresión posparto, ansiedad o llanto sin causa aparente.

2. It is normal and usually transitory.
Es normal y usualmente transitorio.

3. It has been related to the demands of a newborn, tiredness and hormonal imbalances.
Se ha relacionado con las demandas del recién nacido, el cansancio y el desbalance hormonal.

4. Look for professional help if the depression does not improve with time.
Busque ayuda profesional si la depresión no se mejora con el tiempo.

IX. DANGER SIGNS
(Síntomas de Aviso de Peligro)

1. Call your doctor immediately if . . .
Llame a su doctor inmediatamente si . . .

2. you have a fever (with or without chills).
tenga fiebre con o sin escalofríos.

3. you have excessive bleeding or pain with bleeding.
tenga sangrado excesivo o mucho dolor al sangrar.

4. Heavy bleeding would be two wet pads in thirty minutes.
Un sangrado excesivo sería empapar dos toallas sanitarias en treinta minutos.

5. you pass a clot larger than a lemon.
expulse un coágulo mayor que el tamaño de un limón.

6. vaginal bleeding returns to a bright red color after having turned to a brown color.
tenga sangrado vaginal rojo intenso después de haber cambiado al color marrón.

7. you have excessive dizziness.
tenga muchos mareos.

8. there is a strong odor or heavy vaginal discharge.
haya un olor fuerte o mucha descarga vaginal.

9. you have pain or swelling in the chest, abdomen, pelvis or legs.
tenga dolor o hinchazón en el pecho, abdomen, pelvis o piernas.

10. you have marked weakness or fatigue.
tenga una debilidad marcada o mucha fatiga.

MOTHER / INFANT CARE AND POSTPARTUM RECOVERY
The Benefits of Breastfeeding

1. Mother's milk is the best food for your newborn.
La leche materna es el mejor alimento para su recién nacido.

2. Mother's milk helps your baby grow healthy and strong.
La leche materna ayuda a que su bebé crezca sano y fuerte.

3. It helps protect the baby against colds, earaches and other illnesses.
Ayuda a proteger a su bebé contra los resfriados, dolores de oído, y otras enfermedades.

4. It is easily digested.
Se digiere fácilmente.

5. Your baby will have less colic, constipation, and diarrhea.
Su bebé tendrá menos cólico, estreñimiento, y diarrea.

6. Breastfeeding helps return the uterus to its normal size.
Dar el pecho ayuda a que el útero regrese a su tamaño normal.

7. You will get back into shape faster.
Recuperará la forma más rápido.

8. Breastfeeding burns 500 calories a day!
¡Dar pecho quema quinientas calorías por día!

9. Night feedings and travel with the baby are quicker and easier.
Las alimentaciones nocturnas y los viajes con el bebé son más rápidos y sencillos.

10. Breastfeeding economizes money.
Dar el pecho economiza dinero.

11. Breastfeeding develops a special intimacy between you and your baby.
Al dar el pecho se desarrolla un apego especial entre usted y su bebé.

12. The first "milk" that comes from the breast is called colostrum.
La primera "leche" que sale de los senos se llama calostro.

13. Even though it doesn't look like milk, colostrum is very rich in food value.
Aunque no parece leche, el calostro tiene un valor alimenticio muy alto.

MOTHER / INFANT CARE AND POSTPARTUM RECOVERY
Nursing Your Baby

1. Get in a comfortable position.
Póngase en una posición cómoda.

2. I am going to show you the cradle hold.
Le voy a enseñar la posición de cuna.

3. Put the baby to your breast.
Ponga su bebé al pecho.

4. Hold the baby close to your body, stomach to stomach.
Sostenga al bebé cerca de su cuerpo, estómago contra estómago.

5. Support your arm with a pillow.
Sostenga el brazo con una almohada.

6. Lift your breast to the baby's mouth.
Levante el seno hasta la boca del bebé.

7. Lightly touch your nipple to the baby's lower lip until he opens his mouth.
Con el pezón, toque ligeramente el labio inferior del bebé hasta que abra la boca.

8. Center your nipple and areola as far in the baby's mouth as possible.
Centre el pezón y la areola lo más que se pueda dentro de la boca del bebé.

9. The baby's mouth should be covering the brown part of the nipple.
La boca del bebé debe estar bien abierto alrededor del área del pezón.

10. Let the baby suck.
Déjelo chupar.

11. You will feel soft pressure or pulling when the baby sucks.
Sentirá una presión suave o un jaloncito cuando el bebé chupe.

12. Change to the other breast.
Cambie al otro seno (pecho).

13. Gently push one of your fingers into the corner of the baby's mouth.
Suavemente, introduzca un dedo en el ángulo de la boca del bebé.

14. This will break the suction and prevent the baby from biting the nipple.
Esto rompe la succión e impide que el bebé muerda el pezón.

15. Burp the baby before changing to the other breast.
Sáquele los gases del bebé antes de cambiarlo al otro seno.

16. Let the father help burp the baby.
Deje que el padre ayude en sacar los gases del bebé.

17. This will give him an important role in the feeding of his baby.
Eso le da un papel importante en la alimentación de su bebé.

18. Try another position.
Trate otra posición.

19. Lie on the bed with your baby, stomach to stomach.
Acuéstese en la cama con su bebé, estómago contra estómago.

20. The lying-down position is good when you are nursing at night and want to sleep.
La posición acostada es buena cuando está lactando al bebé de noche y desea dormir.

21. And when you need to lie flat after a cesarean delivery.
Y cuando necesita estar completamente acostada después de una cesárea.

22. The football hold is best when . . .
La posición en que sostiene al bebé como una pelota de fútbol americano es preferible cuando

23. . . . your baby is very small or premature.
. . . *su bebé es pequeño o prematuro.*

24. . . . your baby has trouble getting enough of your breast in the mouth.
. . . su bebé tiene problemas en introducir suficiente parte del seno en la boca.

25. . . . you've had a cesarean and don't want the baby to rest on your stiches.
. . . ha tenido una cesárea y no desea que el bebé repose sobre los puntos.

26. . . . you have large breasts.
. . . tiene senos grandes.

27. After nursing, leave your nipples exposed to air until they're dry.
Después de lactar a su bebé, deje los pezones expuestos al aire hasta que estén secos.

28. Air-drying helps keep your nipples healthy.
Esto ayuda a mantener sanos los pezones.

MOTHER / INFANT CARE AND POSTPARTUM RECOVERY
Suggestions for Successful Breastfeeding

1. Begin to breastfeed your newborn as soon as possible.
Empiece a dar el pecho a su recién nacido tan pronto como sea posible.

2. This stimulates the let-down of the milk.
Esto estimula la bajada de la leche.

3. Drink a big glass of water, juice or milk every time you nurse.
Cada vez que dé el pecho, tome un vaso grande de agua, jugo o leche.

4. Nurse often, every one and a half to two hours in the first few weeks.
Lacte frecuentemente a su bebé, cada hora y media hasta dos horas durante las primeras semanas.

5. As your baby gets older, the times between feedings will get longer.
A medida que el bebé crece, aumentará el tiempo entre alimentación y alimentación.

6. The more you nurse, the more milk your body will produce.
Mientras más lacte al bebé, más leche producirá el cuerpo.

7. Nurse your baby when he starts to show signs of hunger.
Alimente a su bebé cuando empieza a darle señales de tener hambre.

8. When babies are hungry they move their mouths and suck on their hands.
Cuando un bebé tiene hambre mueve la boca y se chupan las manitos.

9. Do not wait until your baby cries to feed him.
No espere hasta que llore su bebé para alimentarlo.

10. Let your baby nurse as long as he wants to.
Permita que su bebé lacte por el tiempo que quiera.

11. Babies usually nurse between ten to thirty minutes.
Los bebés normalmente lactan entre diez a treinta minutos.

12. Your baby will either stop nursing or fall asleep at the breast when he is satisfied.
Su bebé dejará de lactar o se quedará dormido cuando esté satisfecho.

13. Avoid giving your baby bottles during the first four to six weeks.
Evite dar biberones (P.R.) teteras (México) a su bebé durante las primeras cuatro a seis semanas.

14. Combining the bottle with the breast may confuse your baby.
El combinar dar pecho con dar tetera puede confundir a su bebé.

15. Your baby does not need formula if you are breastfeeding.
Su bebé no necesita fórmula si le está dando pecho.

16. If your baby wets between six to eight diapers a day and has two bowel movements per day, he is getting enough milk.
Si su bebé moja de seis a ocho pañales al día y evacua los intestinos dos veces al día, está tomando suficiente leche.

17. Remember, the more you nurse your baby, the more milk you will produce.
Recuerde, mientras más le da el pecho a su bebé, más leche producirá.

18. Take good care of yourself.
Cuídese mucho.

19. Drink plenty of liquids.
Tome mucho líquido.

20. Eat nutritious foods.
Coma alimentos nutritivos.

21. Get enough calories.
Obtenga suficientes calorías.

22. Get enough rest.
Descanse lo suficiente.

MOTHER / INFANT CARE AND POSTPARTUM RECOVERY
Alleviating Common Breast Discomforts

1. It is common to have swollen and sore breasts a few days after the baby is born.
Es común tener los senos hinchados y adoloridos unos cuantos días después del parto.

2. Just before nursing, squeeze out some milk until the nipple area gets soft.
Justo antes de lactar, saque leche del seno hasta que el área del pezón se suavice.

3. Place warm towels on your breasts before nursing.
Colóquese toallas tibias sobre los senos antes de dar pecho.

4. Put an ice pack on your breasts after nursing.
Colóquese una bolsa de hielo sobre los senos después de dar pecho.

5. Wear a supportive cotton bra day and night.
Use un sostén de algodón que soporte bien durante el día y la noche.

6. Your nipples may be a little sore in the first few weeks of nursing your baby.
Es posible que los pezones estén un poco adoloridos durante las primeras semanas de lactar a su bebé.

7. To ease the discomfort you can . . .
Para aliviarse usted puede . . .

8. Change nursing positions often.
Varie frecuentemente las posiciones en que da pecho a su bebé.

9. Nurse more often, so the baby is not so hungry at the start of each feeding.
Dele el pecho al bebé más frecuentemente para que no esté tan hambriento al principio de cada alimentación.

10. Begin each nursing with the breast that's least sore.
Comience con el seno que esté menos adolorido.

11. Make sure your baby takes your nipple far enough in the mouth.
Asegúrese de que el pezón esté suficientemente introducido dentro de la boca del bebé.

12. Wet your nipples with some breast milk and let them air dry.
Frote los pezones con un poco de leche materna y permita que se sequen con el aire.

MOTHER/INFANT CARE AND POSTPARTUM RECOVERY
Language Activities and Study Guide

Instructions: Set your own timeframe for the following activities. It is recommended that a beginning learner allow three months for this unit, dedicating approximately 30 minutes a day to the goal of learning Spanish for postpartum care.

Unit 4 Begin Date: _____
Projected End Date: _____

A. Targeted Grammar and Structure: Desea

Once again we will be focusing on a key verb to facilitate your assimilation of terminology pertinent to initial postpartum and newborn care. The key verb for this section is:

¿Desea?   (day.**say**.ah)   Would you like?

Identify all the expressions used with *¿desea?* on pages 117-119 of your text. Then, listen to the phrases from pages 117-119 of your text on the audio program. Repeat after the instructor in Spanish. Listen for the key phrases with the verb *¿desea?* Recognizing key phrases will help you to gain confidence in your ability to hear and reproduce Spanish.

Now create five original sentences with the key verb *desea* relevant to the postpartum care that you offer.

1. ¿Desea _____?
2. ¿Desea _____?
3. ¿Desea _____?
4. ¿Desea _____?
5. ¿Desea _____?

B. Targeted Grammar and Structure: Formal Commands

In order to communicate instructions appropriate to postpartum care, you need to be able to form commands in Spanish. In order to convey a message of respect, we are going to offer advice and communicate instructions using the formal you (*usted*) form. When you have become more familiar with your client, you may switch to the informal *(tú)* form. The grammar for constructing commands in the *usted* (formal you) form is simple. The rule is the following:

Rule:

Verbs in Spanish end in one of three ways: ar, er, ir. Example: tom**ar** (to take), com**er** (to eat) and viv**ir** (to live).

To form commands using *usted* (formal you) there are three simple rules:

a. if a verb ends in **ar** (hablar) remove the **ar** and add **e** and you will have the command.

    Example: evit**ar** --- evit --- evit**e** (avoid)

b. if a verb ends in **er** (comer) remove the **er** and add **a**

    Example: com**er** --- com --- com**a** (eat)

c. if a verb ends in **ir** (vivir) remove the **ir** and add **a**

    Example: viv**ir** --- viv --- viv**a** (live)

Note: Above is the rule. There are always exceptions. In Spanish you will find many irregular commands. There is no way for you to know which verbs conjugate as irregular commands except through usage and by referring to a verb book for verification.

The following are 12 key command forms you will need to guide a new mom through her hospital discharge instructions:

consulte: (cone.**sool**.tay): consult
use: (**oo**.say): use
haga: (**ah**.ga): make
limite: (lim.**ee**.tay): limit
aumente: (owh.**men**.tay): increase
acepte: (ah.**sept**.tay): accept
comience: (coe.me.**yen**.say): begin
evite: (ee.**bee**.tay): avoid
no levante: (no lay.**bon**.tay): don't lift
no maneje: (no maan.**ay**.hay): don't drive
descanse: (des.**con**.say): rest
tome: (**toe**.may): take

Practice these commands several times, following the phonetic pronunciation guide provided above. Learn these words and make them a part of your working vocabulary. By memorizing these 12 commands, and joining them with the appropriate vocabulary, you will be well on your way to communicating with Spanish-speaking moms about their postpartum care.

C. Key Phrases Part I

Next, listen to the structures presented on pages 120-129 of your text on the audio program. As you listen, repeat after the instructor in Spanish as directed. Try to imitate the pronunciation as closely as you can. Listen for the vocabulary and commands you already know. This will give you confidence when you begin to recognize familiar structures. Repeat this exercise as often as needed to impress these phrases on your memory.

Select 25 phrases from those presented on pages 120-129 which you believe to be most valuable to your work. Write them down separately on 3 x 5 index cards (one phrase per card with the Spanish on one side, English on another). These cards will serve as a reference and learning tool. Carry them with you on the job and refer to them when needed. Study them when on break, at lunch, or whenever you have a few free moments in your schedule.

Practice the 25 phrases you have selected until you are comfortable with the pronunciation and the words flow smoothly. When you are comfortable with the pronunciation, read the sentences into a recorder. Replay your recording and listen for any pronunciation errors.

D. Targeted Grammar and Structure: Formal Commands (Continued)

In this section you will be guiding a new mother in breastfeeding her newborn. You will be using commands to communicate your advice. Refer to the grammar rules presented in this lesson for guidance. The following are a few key commands for breastfeeding.

ponga (**pohn**.gah): put or place
sostenga (soos.**tang**.gah): hold or support
acuéstese: (ah.**quest**.tay.say): lie down
toque: (**toe**.kay): touch
levante: (lay.**bon**. tay): lift
levántese: (lay **bon**.tay.say): lift yourself or get up
limpie: (**lim**. pee.aye): clean
límpiese: (**lim**. pee.aye.say): clean yourself
deje: (**day**.hay): leave
dé palmaditas: (**day**. pall. mah. dee.tahs): pat
sobe: (**so**.bay): rub
coloque: (coe.**low**.kay): place
alimente: (ah.lee.**men**.tay): feed or nourish
evite: (a.**bee**.tay): avoid
beba: (**bay**.bah): drink
coma: (**coe**.mah): eat
descanse: (des.**kan**.say): rest
amamante: (ah.mah.**man**.tay): nurse
saque: (**sah**.kay): remove or squeeze out
use: (**ooh**.say): use
varie: (**vah**.ree.aye): change or vary
comience: (coe.me.**en**.say): begin
asegúrese: (ah.say.**goor**.ah.say): make sure
permita: (pear.**me**.tah): allow

Practice these commands several times, following the phonetic pronunciation guide provided above. Learn these words and make them a part of your working vocabulary. By memorizing these commands and joining them with the appropriate vocabulary, you will be well on your way to communicating with new Spanish-speaking moms about breastfeeding options and care.

E. Key Phrases Part II

Listen to the structures on pages 130-141 of your text on the audio program. These phrases provide general knowledge about breastfeeding to the new mom. Linguistically, these phrases are difficult to break down into component parts and therefore must be learned through memorization. The most efficient way to do this is to listen several times to this lesson on the audio program and then to produce the language yourselves by repeating out loud after the instructor. Repetition will be the key to your success. Listen to the vocabulary and commands you already know. This will give you confidence when you begin to recognize familiar structures. Repeat this exercise as often as needed to impress these phrases on your memory.

F. Language Learning Activities

Select 25 phrases from those presented on pages 130-141 which you believe to be most valuable to your work. Write them down separately on 3 x 5 index cards (one phrase per card with the Spanish on one side, English on another). These cards will serve as a reference for you and can be taken on the job and referred to in case of need. This activity helps you to become an active participant in your language training. Practice the 25 phrases you have selected until you are comfortable with the pronunciation and the words flow smoothly. Then, read the sentences into a recorder. Replay your recording and listen for any pronunciation errors.

Cultural Reading
Postpartum Myths and Taboos

The area of postpartum recovery and breastfeeding poses a significant challenge to healthcare professionals as it presents a vast array of cultural myths and taboos, many of which are rooted in folk traditions and ancient healing practices.

In many traditional cultures, both the new mother and the newborn are considered weak and vulnerable after birth. In both Mexico and Puerto Rico, generations of young women have observed *La Cuarentena*, a 40-day rest period during which the new mother stays mostly in bed, or at least at home, and observes special practices which avoid exposure to cold air and/or liquids.

In accordance with the hot and cold tradition, many new moms will refuse to take a shower after childbirth, believing that they have a "hot" wound in the uterus which should not be exposed to the cold, even if only for the brief moment in which she is stepping into or out of the shower. Hair is not to be washed either, for the same fear of exposure to cold air. She will take a sponge bath, however, if most of the body remains covered and unexposed to the air.

As the woman believes that her wound is classified as "hot," she will not expose her sore body to cold of any kind. A "hot" illness or wound can traditionally only be treated with a "hot" remedy. Ice packs for perineal swelling or hemorrhoids will most likely be declined. On the other hand, a warm compress may be welcomed with great relief and gratitude. Cold drinks will probably not be taken, but any kind of hot tea, especially chamomile or mint, will be appreciated.

According to traditional birth customs in Guatemala, soon after the birth the mother eats hot chocolate and sweet bread. She does not get out of bed for 24 hours. The only fluids she takes are hot chocolate, hot water and chamomile tea. It is considered dangerous to drink water at room temperature because there is a wound inside the uterus, and it is harmed by "cold" ingested substances. During postpartum, the mothers mostly eat chicken and tortillas. If a woman is very poor, she basically eats only tortillas and rice. She doesn't take milk, eggs, beans, avocados, and fruits because these are considered "cold" foods. Some women eat almost nothing for ear of doing harm to themselves or their baby."

Fear of causing harm to the baby is a common concern for new mothers and their families. Every precaution is taken to protect the newborn from what traditional cultures call the "evil eye," in Spanish known as *el mal de ojo*.

In the Mexican tradition, newborns are protected with a string around the wrist or a coin binding the belly button. In Puerto Rico, infants are protected with a tiny bracelet called *la pulserita de la hasabache,* or *los ojitos de Santa Lucia.* Santa Lucia is the patron saint and protector of children.

If the tradition does not cause any major health risk, let the family be comforted by it. If a practice is a potential risk, inform and educate the family, in as gentle a manner as possible.

For example, if you fear that the coin may cause an infection say, *Yo sé que es una tradición suya. Es importante asegurar que la moneda no se infecte al cordón. Si lo va a dejar allí, por lo menos quítele la moneda cada vez que cambie el pañal y limpie el cordón con alcohol.*

By responding in such a manner, you have demonstrated sensitivity, an awareness of cross-cultural understanding, moderation, and grace in dealing with a cultural practice foreign to your own. Such are the qualities that will make any cross-cultural interaction a success.

Be culturally astute when caring for a Hispanic newborn. Try not to admire a newborn without touching him and/or invoking God's blessing over him. In Puerto Rico, it is believed that the curse of the evil eye will be inflicted if a baby is complimented without invoking God's blessing. Always follow a compliment with *Qué Diós lo bendiga.* (May God bless him).

According to Mexican folklore, a baby that is admired and not touched will become cursed with the evil eye. Many nurses have wondered why some Hispanic mothers have tried so desperately to get them to hold or caress their newborn baby. It is possible that these nurses might have said something like, *¡Qué bebé más lindo!* or *¡Qué ojos más bellos!* Without having touched the baby.

Once the baby is cursed with the evil eye, only the one who put the curse on that baby can remove it. Remember, if you want to compliment a baby, wash your hands first and then immediately touch or hold the newborn. Do not leave the room, or even worse your shift, without being culturally-sensitive to the curse of the evil eye.

Of all the myths, fears and misunderstanding about the nature and value of breastfeeding, colostrum presents the first stumbling block to successful nursing within the Latin community.

The value and benefits of colostrum are all too often misunderstood. Many Hispanic women have been told by their mothers and their mothers before them that colostrum is of poor quality and even damaging food for a newborn. Until the milk comes in, the baby is often fed olive oil, herbal teas, sugar water, weak coffee, and of course formula.

And as they wait for their milk to come in, mothers in Puerto Rico are often *fed sopa de gandules* (pigeon pea soup) to increase their milk supply.

A new mother may listen politely as you tell her about the benefits of breastfeeding, almost convincing you that you have gotten through with your message. However, you may later learn that your attentive patient has decided to bottle feed her baby, at least while she is in the hospital, she says. She has promised to begin nursing as soon as she is in the comfort of her own home and, of course, when her milk comes in.

This does not happen in all cases, by any means. Many Hispanic women, especially those who share ethnicity with indigenous Indian populations of Mexico and Guatemala, are very natural and comfortable with nursing their newborns. Others, however, are not and must be educated and guided to the value and pleasure of breastfeeding a newborn.

Sometimes this lack of education is rooted in cultural myths and taboos, some of which we as childbirth professionals unknowing foster despite our best intentions.

For example, if somewhere in the explanation your patient received about the benefits of breastfeeding, she learned that her breasts were producing a yellowish substance called colostrum, this information may have unknowingly invoked superstition and fear. In the folk culture of some Latin-American villages, yellow is a very inauspicious color. By telling a new mom that she has a yellowish substance with which to nourish her newborn, the potential for inadvertently invoking superstition is high.

Whether fighting superstition or simple reluctance, I would like to suggest a way to work with the cultural barrier presented by the concept of colostrum. Why not just go with her fears and perceptions by letting the new mom pump her breasts to extract the colostrum, getting to the milk a bit faster. And don´t even mention color, just refer to the colostrum as a creamy white substance full of nutrition and value. Learn how to work with fears rather than against them and you will be assured of offering more culturally-relevant care to your breastfeeding mom.

Remember, however, that you are going to be fighting against years of misinformation and cultural propaganda. In developing countries, bottle feeding with formula has been glamorized through advertising. It is portrayed as the best way to feed babies and the best way to have a healthy baby.

Striving to provide the best for their babies by following the "Western" ideal, many mothers begin formula feeding their babies by using the free supplies that are given out at hospitals and clinics. But once these supplies run out, families are often unable to afford the high cost of purchasing formula. Meanwhile, the mother's milk has dried up. So the expensive formula is watered down to stretch its use for as long as possible, causing malnutrition.

Also, as preparation instructions are usually in English, the formula is often prepared incorrectly. Malnutrition is the least tragic result of inadequate preparation and education.

You can begin now to reverse this cultural trend toward the status symbol of the bottle by providing culturally-relevant education and information to clients of all social, ethnic and cultural backgrounds. *After my milk comes in* can become *when my colostrum comes in*. All it takes is a little education.

Questions for Discussion

1. What myths, fears and misunderstandings have you encountered in the area of breastfeeding or postpartum care among your Latin clients?

2. What percentage of Latin moms would you project actually breastfeed their newborns?

Unit Five
NEONATAL INTENSIVE CARE

Communicating with the Parents
Introduction to the Unit
Care of your Baby in NICU
Common Neonatal Medical Problems
Taking Your Baby Home
In the Hands of God

NEONATAL INTENSIVE CARE
Communicating With The Parents

1. Your baby is in critical condition.
Su bebé está en una condición crítica.

2. Your baby is very sick.
Su bebé está muy enfermo.

3. Your baby is in the Neonatal Intensive Care Unit.
Su bebé está en la Unidad de Cuidado Neonatal Intensivo.

4. Your baby needs to be transferred to another hospital.
Su bebé necesita ser transferido a otro hospital.

5. This experience may be a little difficult for you.
Puede que esta experiencia sea un poquito difícil para ustedes.

6. We are here to help you and your baby.
Estamos aquí para ayudarle a usted y a su bebé.

7. This is the neonatalogist, Dr. Suárez.
Este es el neonatólogo, el Dr. Suárez.

8. He will take very good care of your baby.
El cuidará de una forma muy especial a su bebé.

9. Your baby will receive special care twenty-four hours a day.
Su bebé recibirá cuidado especial durante las veinticuatro horas del día.

10. The doctor is going to perform various tests on your baby.
El doctor va a realizar varias pruebas a su bebé.

11. He will examine your baby's heart, blood pressure, breathing, and temperature.
Examinará el corazón, la presión sanguínea, la respiración y la temperatura de su bebé.

12. The doctor needs an x-ray of your baby's chest.
El doctor necesita una placa del pecho de su bebé.

13. This is Ramón, the x-ray technician.
Este es Ramón, el técnico de radiografía.

14. He is going to take the x-ray.
El tomará la placa.

15. The doctor needs to do a spinal tap (a spinal test) on your baby.
El doctor necesita hacerle una punción lumbar (una prueba espinal) a su bebé.

16. Please sign this consent form.
Firme este formulario de consentimiento, por favor.

17. Your baby needs an operation.
Su bebé necesita una operación.

18. Your baby needs surgery.
Su bebé necesita cirugía.

19. We are preparing him for surgery now.
Lo estamos preparando para cirugía ahora.

20. This is the anesthesiologist.
Este es el anestesiólogo.

21. He will administer general anesthesia to your baby.
Administrará anestesia general a su bebé.

22. The baby will be asleep during the surgery.
El bebé estará dormido durante la cirugía.

23. He will not feel any pain.
No sentirá ningún dolor.

24. Your baby is dying.
Su bebé está muriéndose.

25. His condition has changed.
Su condición ha cambiado.

26. Come to the hospital and see him.
Vengan al hospital a verlo.

27. ¿Would you like to baptize your baby?
¿Desea bautizar a su bebé?

28. ¿Would you like to talk to a priest? Pastor? Nun?
¿Desea hablar con un sacerdote? Un pastor? Una monja?

29. I am so sorry.
Lo siento tanto.

30. We did all we could do for your baby.
Se hizo todo lo posible por su bebé.

31. But, it was impossible to save him.
Pero, fue imposible salvarlo.

32. Sadly, your baby has died.
Lamentablemente, su bebé falleció.

33. ¿Would you like to see him?
¿Desea verlo?

34. ¿Would you like to hold him?
¿Desea cogerlo (Puerto Rico) cargarlo (México)?

35. ¿Would you like to take his footprints as a memory?
¿Desea llevar sus huellitas a casa como un recuerdo?

36. ¿Would you like a lock of his hair?
¿Desea quedarse con un pedacito de su pelo?

37. ¿Would you like to keep his bracelet?
¿Desea quedarse con su brazalete?

38. ¿Would you like a photo of your baby?
¿Desea una foto de su bebé?

NEONATAL INTENSIVE CARE
Introduction to the Unit

1. Your first visit to NICU may be a little frightening.
Su primera visita a NICU puede causarle un poco de miedo.

2. Your baby may seem fragile.
Su bebé puede parecerle frágil.

3. He may not look like you imagined.
Puede que no aparezca como usted lo imaginaba.

4. NICU is a very active place.
NICU es un lugar muy activo.

5. Don't be frightened if you hear alarms.
No se asuste si escucha alarmas.

6. They come from the equipment that is used to monitor the progress of your baby.
Vienen del equipo que se usa para vigilar el progreso de su bebé.

7. This vigilance is the reason for all the wires and tubes.
Esa vigilancia es la razón para tener muchos de los cables y tubitos.

8. They do not cause pain to your baby.
No causan dolor a su bebé.

9. I am going to explain the purpose of each piece of equipment to you.
Les voy a explicar el propósito de cada pieza de este equipo.

10. It is important that you get involved in your baby's care.
Es importante que ustedes como padres se envuelvan en el cuidado que recibe su bebé.

11. Your baby needs a lot of loving care.
Su bebé necesita mucho cariño y amor.

12. We are going to visit him now.
Vamos a visitarlo ahora.

13. There are a few procedures that you must observe before visiting your baby.
Hay algunos procedimientos que debe seguir antes de visitar a su bebé.

14. Please wash your hands.
Lávese las manos, por favor.

15. Remove all of your jewelry.
Quítese todas las prendas.

16. Put on this gown.
Póngase esta bata.

17. Put on this mask.
Póngase esta mascarilla.

18. These precautions protect your baby from infection.
Estas precauciones protegen a su bebé contra las infecciones

19. You may bring a few toys for your baby.
Puede traer unos cuantos juguetes para su bebé.

20. Do not bring stuffed animals.
No traiga peluches.

21. The baby will like bright colors.
Al bebé le gustarán los colores brillantes.

22. You can bring music, photos of the family, or a recording of your voice.
Puede traer música, fotos de la familia, o una grabación de su voz.

23. Your baby will start to recognize your voice and your touch.
Su bebé aprenderá reconocer su voz y su toque.

24. The most important gift you can give your baby is your love.

El regalo más importante que usted puede darle a su bebé es su cariño.

25. You are one of the most important factors in your baby's recovery.
Ustedes son uno de los factores más importantes en la recuperación de su bebé.

26. Sit next to your baby's crib.
Siéntese al lado de la cuna de su bebé.

27. Touch her.
Tóquela.

28. Gently put your finger in your baby's hand.
Coloque su dedo suavemente en la manito de su bebé.

29. Talk to her softly.
Háblele suavemente.

30. The baby likes to hear your voice.
Al bebé le gusta oír su voz.

31. Don't hesitate to ask any question you may have.
No dude en hacer cualquier pregunta que tenga.

32. It doesn't matter how silly the question may seem.
No importa cuán tonta parezca la pregunta.

33. We are here to help you.
Estamos aquí para servirle.

34. It is very important that you have peace of mind.
Es muy importante que usted tenga tranquilidad mental.

35. We understand your doubts and fears.
Comprendemos sus inquietudes y temores.

NEONATAL INTENSIVE CARE
Care of your Baby in NICU

A. Monitoring Your Baby
(Monitorizando a su Bebé)

1. Your baby is connected to a cardiac monitor that registers his vital signs.
Su bebé está conectado a un monitor cardiaco que registra los signos vitales.

2. Vital signs are registered through these patches on his chest and left leg.
Se registran los signos vitales a través de los parchos colocados en el pecho y muslo izquierdo.

3. The monitor measures arterial pressure, respirations per minute and blood oxygen levels.
El monitor mide la presión arterial, las respiraciones por minuto y los niveles de oxígeno en la sangre.

4. Your baby is suffering from bradycardia.
Su bebé padece de la bradicardia.

5. Bradycardia means a slower than normal heartbeat.
Bradicardia significa latidos menos de lo normal en el corazón.

6. This heart monitor alerts the nurse when the heartbeat slows down or speeds up.

Este monitor cardíaco alerta a la enfermera cuando los latidos del corazón están bajos o altos.

B. Keeping Your Baby Warm
(Manteniendo Caliente a su Bebé)

1. Your premature baby does not have enough fat to keep himself warm.
Su bebé prematuro no tiene suficiente grasa para mantenerse caliente.

2. To keep him warm we will place him in this incubator/warmer.
Para darle más calor, lo colocaremos en este incubadora / calentador.

3. The incubator simulates the warm, cozy environment of a mother's womb.
La incubadora ofrece al recién nacido un ambiente cálido muy parecido al del vientre materno.

4. This thermometer attached to the baby's skin connects to the warmer.
Este termómetro pegadito a la piel del bebé se conecta al calentador.

5. The thermometer turns on when the baby is too cold and shuts of when he is warm.
El termómetro se prende cuando el bebé está demasiado frío y se apaga cuando está caliente.

C. Helping Your Baby to Breath
(Ayudando a su Bebé Respirar)

1. It is common that premature babies have trouble breathing.
Es común que los bebés prematuros tengan problemas de respiración.

2. Their lungs are not fully developed.
Sus pulmones no están completamente maduros todavía.

3. Your baby has apnea.
Su bebé tiene apnea.

4. He occasionally stops breathing.
Ocasionalmente deja de respirar.

5. We are going to put your baby on a respirator to help him breathe.
Le vamos a poner a su bebé en un ventilador para ayudarle a respirar.

6. This sensory device will sound when your baby stops breathing.
Este dispositivo sensorial suena cuando su bebé deja de respirar.

7. This small tube connected to the respirator is delivering oxygen to your baby.
Este tubito conectado a la máquina le da oxígeno a su bebé.

8. Your baby has broncopulmonary dysplasia.
Su bebé tiene displasia broncopulmonar.

9. He needs oxygen.
Necesita oxígeno.

10. This mask will give oxygen to your baby.
Esta máscara le dará oxígeno a su bebé.

11. Your baby has RDS (Respiratory Distress Syndrome)
Su bebé tiene RDS (Síndrome de Distrés Respiratorio).

12. His lungs are weak.
Sus pulmones están débiles.

13. We will put him under this oxihood until he can breathe on his own.
Le colocaremos debajo de este "oxihood" hasta que pueda respirar por si mismo.

14. The oxygen flows into the hood through this tube.
El oxígeno fluye dentro de la cabaña a través de éste tubito.

15. This machine is called a mechanical ventilator.
Esta máquina se llama un ventilador mecánico.

16. It will deliver oxygen to your baby's lungs.
Llevará oxígeno a los pulmones de su bebé.

17. This nasal tube is placed in the nose and gives your baby a steady flow of oxygen to the lungs.
Este tubito nasal se coloca en la nariz y le da a su bebé un flujo continuo de oxígeno hasta los pulmones.

18. This tube is inserted into your baby's mouth and trachea (endotracheal tube).
Este tubito se pasa por la boca y la tráquea de su bebé (tubo endotraqueal).

19. The tube is connected to a machine that pumps air into the lungs.
El tubo se conecta a una máquina que bombea aire dentro de los pulmones.

20. This tube is used to remove mucousy substances from the nose, throat and trachea.
Este tubito se usa para remover las substancias mucosas de la nariz, garganta o tráquea.

21. We will give your baby a medicine called surfactant to help develop his lungs.
Le administraremos una medicina que se llama surfactant a su bebé para ayudarle madurar sus pulmoncitos.

D. Feeding Your Premature Baby
(Alimentando a Su Bebé Prematuro)

1. Your premature baby may not be able to nurse for many days, weeks or months.
Su bebé prematuro puede no poder lactar por varios días, semanas, o meses.

2. Your baby does not yet know how to suck or swallow.
Su bebé no sabe todavía como chupar o tragar.

3. We will nourish him through this I.V pump.
Le alimentaremos por medio de esta máquina de suero.

4. He will receive nourishment through this catheter needle positioned in his vein.
Recibirá los nutrientes por medio de este pequeño catéter colocada en la vena.

5. The fluids he is receiving through the I.V. contain nutritious substances.
Los líquidos que recibe del suero contienen substancias nutritivas.

6. The quantity of liquid that your baby receives is carefully calculated.
La cantidad de líquidos que recibe su bebé se mide cuidadosamente.

7. This tube attached to his belly button is giving your baby fluids and medicine.
Este tubito que está introducido en el ombligo está dando líquidos y medicina a su bebé.

8. It is also used to extract small amounts of blood and to measure blood pressure.
Se lo usa también para extraer pequeñas cantidades de sangre y para medir la presión sanguínea.

9. When the baby gets better, he can receive nourishment through a nasal tube.
Cuando el bebé se mejore, puede recibir la alimentación por un tubo nasal.

10. When your baby is even stronger, he can begin to nurse or receive the bottle.
Cuando su bebé esté aún más fuerte, puede comenzar a lactar o tomar el biberón.

11. If you want to nurse, you need to pump your breasts and store the expressed milk.
Si desea lactar, necesita extraer la leche de su seno y guardarla para más tarde.

12. I can show you how to use the hospital's electric pump.
Le puedo enseñar como usar la bomba eléctrica del hospital.

13. Wash your hands.
Lave las manos.

14. Drink some water, juice or milk.
Tome algo de agua, jugo o leche.

15. Breathe deeply to relax yourself.
Respire profundo para relajarse.

16. Put a warm towel on your breasts.
Coloca una toallita caliente sobre los senos.

17. Massage your breasts to help the milk flow.
Dé un masaje a los senos para ayudar a que fluya la leche.

18. Adjust the pump so that it begins slowly.
Ajuste la bomba para que empiece despacio.

19. Increase the speed until you are at a comfortable level.
Vaya aumentando hasta alcanzar el nivel más cómodo para usted.

20. Place your breast in the middle of the unit.
Coloque el seno en el centro del receptáculo.

21. Pull the unit away from you to imitate the rhythm in which the baby sucks.
Jale suavemente el receptáculo hacia afuera para imitar el ritmo con que el bebé mama.

22. Your milk will come out in drops at first.
Al principio la leche va a salir en gotitas.

23. Then there will be a gush of milk.
Después habrá una chorrea de leche.

24. Extract milk for ten to fifteen minutes from each breast
Extráigase leche por diez a quince minutos en cada seno.

25. Try to extract milk every two to three hours while you are awake, and one time at night.
Trate de extraerse leche cada dos a tres horas mientras esté despierta, y una vez en la noche.

26. Extracting milk regularly is the only way to maintain your supply.
El extraerse regularmente es la única manera de mantener su provisión de leche.

27. Store your milk in the refrigerator or in the freezer.
Guarde su leche en el refrigerador (México) la nevera (Puerto Rico) o en el congelador.

28. It will keep for two days in the refrigerator and six months in the freezer.
Se mantendrá por dos días en el refrigerador, y seis meses en el congelador.

29. Use a clean, sterile bottle every time you extract milk.
Cada vez que se extraiga leche, utilice un biberón nuevo y estéril.

30. Identify each bottle with the baby's name, date and time of extraction.
Identifique cada envase con el nombre del bebé, la fecha, y la hora de extracción.

31. Do not heat the milk in the microwave or on the stove.
No caliente la leche en el microondas o en la estufa.

32. Leave the frozen milk in the refrigerator overnight.
Deje la leche congelada en el refrigerador la noche anterior.

33. Put the frozen milk in a cup of warm water to unfreeze it.
Ponga la leche congelada en una taza con agua templada para descongelarla.

34. Shake the bottle to mix the milk.
Agite el biberón para mezclar la leche.

NEONATAL INTENSIVE CARE
Common Neonatal Medical Problems

1. Your baby has jaundice.
Su bebé tiene ictericia.

2. Jaundice turns the skin yellow due to an excess of bilirubin in the blood.
La ictericia produce un color amarillento en la piel debido a un aumento de bilirrubina en la sangre.

3. Jaundice is treated with special lights that help eliminate the bilirubin.
Se trata la ictericia con luces especiales que ayudan a eliminar la bilirrubina.

4. Your baby will be without clothes in order to expose his skin to the photo therapy lights.
Su bebé va a estar sin ropa para exponer la piel a las luces de la fototerapia.

5. The lights will not burn his skin.
Las luces no quemarán su piel.

6. I am going to put this mask over his eyes.
Voy a colocar esta máscara sobre sus ojitos.

7. The mask will protect his eyes from the light.
La máscara protegerá sus ojitos de la luz.

8. While he is under the lights his stools will be more frequent, watery and greenish.
Mientras esté bajo las luces, su excreta va a ser más frecuente, aguada y verdosa.

9. Your baby has anemia.
Su bebé tiene anemia.

10. We need to give him a blood transfusion.
Necesitamos ponerle una transfusión de sangre.

11. Do you agree?
¿Está usted de acuerdo?

12. We need to give him vitamins and iron to strengthen his blood.
Necesitamos darle vitaminas y hierro para fortalecer la sangre.

13. Your baby is having convulsions.
Su bebé está convulsando.

14. Your baby has an intraventricular hemorrhage.
Su bebé tiene una hemorragia intraventricular.

15. This means that he is bleeding in the brain.
Esto significa que está sangrando en el cerebro.

16. Your baby has necrotizing enterocolitis (NEC).
Su bebé tiene enterocolitis necrotizante (NEC).

17. NEC is an infection in the intestines that interferes with the digestion and absorption of food.
NEC es una infección en los intestinos que interfiere con la digestión y absorción de alimentos.

18. The infection has caused deterioration of the intestine caused by lack of oxygen.
La infección ha causado deterioro del intestino causado por falta de oxígeno.

19. I am going to give him antibiotics through the I.V. to treat the infection.
Le voy a dar antibióticos por el suero para tratar la infección.

20. The doctor will have to perform surgery to remove the affected portion of the intestine.
El doctor necesita someter a su bebé a una cirugía para remover la porción del intestino afectado.

21. Your baby has pneumonia.
Su bebé tiene pulmonía.

22. I am going to give him antibiotics to eliminate the infection.
Le voy a dar antibióticos para eliminar la infección.

23. Your baby has a blood infection called sepsis.
Su bebé tiene una infección en la sangre que se llama sepsis.

24. Your baby was born with a cleft palate/cleft lip.
Su bebé nació con un paladar hendido/labio leporino.

25. These are facial malformations that occur during the embryonic period.
Estos son unas malformaciones faciales que ocurren durante el desarrollo embrionario.

26. This condition can be corrected through surgery.
Se puede corregir esta condición con cirugía.

NEONATAL INTENSIVE CARE
Taking Your Baby Home

1. Your baby will be ready to go home when . . .
Su bebé estará listo para ir a casa cuando . . .

2. he can breathe on his own, without the help of a ventilator.
pueda respirar por si mismo, sin la ayuda del ventilador.

3. he can keep himself warm, without the use of an incubator.
pueda mantenerse caliente por si mismo, sin la ayuda de una incubadora.

4. his medical condition is stable.
su condición médica sea estable.

5. he is able to nurse or bottle feed.
pueda lactar o alimentarse con un biberón.

6. he weighs approximately four pounds.
pese aproximadamente cuatro libras.

7. Your baby will be transferred to the regular care nursery before being sent home.
Transferiremos a su bebé a la Sala de los Recién Nacidos antes de enviarlo a casa.

8. He can be transferred to a hospital closer to your home.
Se puede transferirlo a un hospital que esté más cerca de su casa.

9. You need to choose a doctor for your baby before he leaves NICU.
Usted necesita escoger un doctor para su bebé antes de que salga de la unidad NICU.

10. We will send a report to your doctor when your baby is discharged.
Le enviaremos un informe al doctor cuando demos de alta a su bebé.

11. Do you have a car seat for your baby?
¿Tiene un asiento protector para su bebé?

12. A car seat is not the same as a baby carrier.
El asiento protector no es lo mismo que el cargador.

13. Federal law requires that all babies be restrained in a car seat.
La ley federal requiere que todos los bebés usen asientos protectores.

NEONATAL INTENSIVE CARE
Language Activities and Study Guide

Instructions: Set your own timeframe for the following activities. It is recommended that a beginning learner allow three months for this unit, dedicating approximately 30 minutes a day to the goal of learning Spanish for prenatal care.

Unit 5 Begin Date: _____
Projected End Date: _____

A. Targeted Grammar and Structure:

The Future Tense

In this section you will be guiding new parents to the complex, often frightening world of Neonatal Intensive Care. A lot of your communication will take place in the future tense. Future tense is one of the simplest verb forms in Spanish. The rule for conjugating in the future tense is as follows:

Rule: to the infinitive (root form) of the verb, add the ending as it is indicted in the column below. Note: -ar, -er, -ir ending verbs are all conjugated the same in the future tense. That's what makes it so easy!

yo (I)	hablaré	comeré	viviré
tu (you)	hablarás	comerás	vivirás
el, ella, usted (he, she, you)	hablará	comerá	vivirá
nosotros (we)	hablaremos	comeremos	viviremos
ellos, ellas, ustedes (they, you)	hablarán	comerán	vivirán

Activity #1: Conjugate the following verbs in the future tense: *recibir* (to receive), *examinar* (to examine), *vigilar* (to watch), *aprender* (to learn), *alimentar* (to feed)

Example: *Estar* (to be)

Yo estaré   (I will be)
Tu estarás   (you will be)
El, ella, usted estará   (he, she, you will be)
Nosotros estaremos   (we will be)
Ellos, ellas, ustedes estarán   (they, you will be)

Activity #2: Identify the verbs used in Activity #1 in the context from which they came. Look for each verb as it is used in one of the phrases found on pages 158-183. Mark the phrase in which each verb appears.

Activity #3: Use each of the 5 verbs in a new, original sentence that has meaning in a neonatal setting.

A. (recibir) _____.

B. (examinar) _____.

C. (vigilar) _____.

D. (aprender) _____.

E. (alimentar) _____.

B. Key Phrases

Listen to the structures presented on pages 158-183 on the audio program. As you listen, repeat after the instructor in Spanish. Try to imitate the pronunciation as closely as you can. Listen for the vocabulary and verb forms you already know. This will give you confidence when you begin to recognize familiar structures. Repeat this exercise as often as needed to impress these phrases on your memory.

Select 25 phrases from those presented on pages 158-183 which you believe to be most valuable to your work. Write them down separately on 3 x 5 index cards (one phrase per card with the Spanish on one side, English on another). These cards will serve as a reference and learning tool. Carry them with you on the job and refer to when needed, as often as needed. Study them when on break, at lunch, or whenever you have a few free moments in your schedule.

Practice the 25 phrases you have selected until you are comfortable with the pronunciation and the words flow smoothly. When you are comfortable with the pronunciation, read the sentences into a recorder. Replay your recording and listen for any pronunciation errors.

Cultural Reading
In the Hands of God

Neonatal death is without a doubt one of the most tragic events a nurse will face in her profession. There is not much you can offer the grieving parents except a kind word, a hug, or a sincere expression of empathy for the pain of a couple who has lost a precious, but too fragile child.

Grief and pain expression are viewed very differently among cultures. American cultural values support a more stoic attitude to grief and mourning, and reveres dignity and silent suffering as we saw so nobly in the face of Jacqueline Kennedy after the loss of her child and then later, her husband. Tears are reserved for the privacy of family and intimate friends.

The Hispanic culture supports a more open, emotional attitude towards grief and loss. Tears are not restricted to the family and close friends; they are shared with many, beginning with those who are around at the time of receiving any bad news. Moral support is offered on many levels, and you as hospital staff will most likely be the first to be able to offer comfort and support during the painful and difficult experience of telling a new mother and father that their baby has died.

What do you say? What do you do to console a weeping mother or a shocked and distant father? While in English this is often a daunting task, how much more so it must be when you don't have the words to offer even the most minimal support in another language. Your attempts will be greatly appreciated, however, no matter how modest your effort may seem.

No matter how much or how little you can say, a hug will be greatly appreciated. Such a simple act of caring will be so meaningful to a grieving mom. The Hispanic culture takes great comfort in touch. If you are not comfortable in hugging, take her hand and hold it in yours for a moment. Place your hand on the father's shoulder and transfer to him the warmth of human compassion.

Ask the grieving couple if they want to see their baby: *¿Desea ver a su bebé?* Ask them if they want to hold him? *¿Desea cogerlo (cargarlo)?* Ask them if they would like an imprint of his footprints to take home as a memory. *¿Desea quedarse con sus huellitas como un recuerdo?* Then ask them if they would like to keep a lock of the baby's hair or his name band. *¿Desea quedarse con un pedacito de su pelo o su brazaleta?*

Offer to take a photo of the baby. *¿Desea una foto de su bebé?* Encourage the father to hold the baby as well. As you know, research has documented that holding the baby will bring a feeling of closeness that otherwise might never occur without your gentle insistence.

Communication with the father is a vital link to the grieving process. He at first may appear angry or unconcerned, cold or distant. If he comes from a traditional Hispanic culture, his *machismo* may not allow him to express much emotion. This is what he has been taught. It is his own cultural value.

On the other hand, he may be tender and affectionate towards the mother of his child, allowing himself to express the flip side of the Hispanic tradition — tenderness and moral support on a very human, very caring level.

As in any culture, there is no set pattern of behavior. What will be overwhelmingly common, however, will be the role the man will be given as decision maker in this time of grief and crisis. This is a role that he is normally comfortable with, and a role which his wife will most likely eagerly concede to him in this time of confusion and helplessness.

When decisions must be made on funeral arrangements, a memorial service, pastoral counsel or whatever decision which will ultimately affect the well-being of the couple, try to make sure that the woman is involved in the decision making. Her natural tendency will probably be to allow her husband to take over, leaving her numb and powerless.

Those who work with mothers suffering the loss of a baby know that she will heal better if she is allowed to take part in some of the initial decision making. Make sure to allow her to express her opinion, even if you have to prod her a bit initially.

For example, if you have asked the couple if they would like to talk to a priest or a pastor, *¿Desean hablar con un sacerdote o un pastor?* and the father says no, ask her again, gently: *¿Está segura?* (Are your sure)? Then ask her if she wants to baptize the baby. *¿Desea bautizar a su bebé?*

The Hispanic population in general has a strong Catholic tradition, especially focused on the Virgin Mary in times of suffering and sorrow. The grieving mother may be comforted by a wallet size image of the Virgin or of Christ that she can hold in her hand as you say: *Tenga esta tarjeta.* (Take this card). *Le traerá confort y paz.* (It will bring you comfort and peace). *Guarde esta oración.* (Keep this prayer). *Le dará valentía y esperanza.* (It will give you valor and hope).

You may also say: *Su bebé está en las manos de Diós.* (Your baby is in the hands of God). *El Señor lo cuidará.* (The Lord will take care of him). You may also place a small guardian angel pin in her hand and say: *Tenga este angelito de la guardia.* (Take this guardian angel). *Velará a su bebé.* (It will watch over your baby). Such simple words, combined with something tangible that has always comforted, may bring one small moment of relief to the hurting mom.

You might also suggest to the father, or another family member, to go down to the gift store and buy a little porcelain or ceramic angel in memory of the baby. You may wish to talk to the gift shop manager at your hospital to have these items available for purchase.

Ceramic items are popular in the Hispanic culture, especially those with a religious theme: little angels, baby Jesus, the Virgin. Encourage the store to stock cards and items with religious themes in Spanish

Offering comfort and support after the death of a newborn is never easy. Armed with a little bit of cultural knowledge, however, and a few lines of comfort in the new language will make all the difference in your approach to the situation. Shocked and grieving parents will at least know that you cared enough to comfort them in their own language. What more precious gift can you give than that of yourself?

Questions for Discussion

1. In your experience, how have you seen pain and mourning expressed in the Hispanic culture? How is it different from the American expression of it?

2. What physical expressions of comfort can you offer the grieving parents?

3. Why is communication with the father a vital link in the grieving process?

4. Why is it important that the mother be involved in the decision-making process regarding the death of her infant and how can you make her a part of that process?

5. What items may help in the grieving process?

Unit Six
WELL WOMAN CARE/GYNECOLOGY

Family Planning and Contraception
Options in Birth Control
The STD Interview
Gynecological Cancer Screening
Menopause
Using *Tener* in the Present Tense
How Cultural Values Affect Gynecological
Decisions

WELL WOMAN CARE AND GYNECOLOGY
Family Planning and Contraception

1. Do you plan to have more children?
¿Piensa tener más hijos?

2. Are you sexually active?
¿Está usted sexualmente activa?

3. Do you have many partners?
¿Tiene muchos compañeros?

4. Have you had many partners in the past?
¿Ha tenido muchos compañeros en el pasado?

5. Do you presently use contraception / birth control?
¿Usa actualmente anticonceptivos / control de nacimiento?

6. The Pill? Condoms? The Diaphragm? The I.U.D.? An injection?

¿La Píldora? ¿Los condones? ¿El diafragma? ¿El Dispositivo Intrauterino (D.I.U.)? ¿Una inyección?

7. Spermicides? The Patch? The Vaginal Ring? The Cervical Cap?
¿Espermicidas? ¿El Parcho? ¿El Anillo Vaginal? ¿La Cubierta Cervical?

8. How long have you used this method?
¿Por cuánto tiempo ha usado este método?

9. Do you like this method?
¿Le gusta éste método?

10. Why did you stop using it?
¿Por qué dejó de usarlo?

11. Do you want to change to a different method?
¿Quiere cambiar a otro método?

12. Have you had a tubal ligation?
¿Se le ataron los tubos?

13. Has he had a vasectomy?
¿Le hicieron a él vasectomía?

WELL WOMAN CARE AND GYNECOLOGY
Options in Birth Control

A. The Pill
(La Píldora Anticonceptiva)

1. The pill is one of the most efficient methods of birth control.
La píldora es uno de los métodos más eficaces para controlar la natalidad.

2. It is one of the easiest methods to use.
Es uno de los métodos más sencillos de usar.

3. In order for the pill to be effective, you have to take one pill a day for 21 (28) days.
Para que la píldora sea eficaz, necesita tomar una pastilla cada día durante 21 (28) días.

4. It is important to take the pill at the same time every day.
Es importante tomar la píldora a la misma hora cada día.

5. If you forget to take a pill, take one as soon as you remember it.
Si se le olvida tomar una píldora, tómela tan pronto se acuerde.

6. Use another method of contraception in addition to avoid pregnancy.
Use un método anticonceptivo adicional para evitar el embarazo.

B. The I.U.D.
(El Dispositivo Intrauterino, D.I.U.)

1. The I.U.D. is a plastic or metal piece which is placed inside the uterus.
El D.I.U. es un artefacto plástico o de metal que se coloca en el interior del útero.

2. It is left in place for an extended period of time (five to ten years).
Se lo deja colocado por un largo periodo de tiempo (cinco a diez años).

3. If you have multiple sex partners, you should not use this method.
Si tiene múltiples parejas sexuales, no debe usar este método.

4. If your husband has other women, you should not use this method.
Si su esposo tiene otras mujeres, no debe usar este método.

5. If you have had a uterine infection, you should not use this method.
Si ha tenido una infección uterina, no debe usar este método.

C. The Diaphragm
(El Diafragma)

1. The diaphragm is placed in the vagina and creates a barrier to the passage of sperm.
El diafragma se coloca en la vagina y crea una barrera al paso del esperma.

2. The diaphragm must always be used with a contraceptive jelly or cream.
Siempre hay que usar el diafragma con una jalea o crema anticonceptiva.

3. If your partner uses a condom, this method is 98% effective.
Si su compañero usa el condón, la eficacia de este método es de un 98% porciento.

4. If you use the diaphragm, it must be refitted after each pregnancy, pelvic surgery, and weight gain greater than ten pounds.
Si usa el diafragma, hay que medirse de nuevo después de cada embarazo, cirugía pélvica, y aumento de peso de más de diez libras.

D. Spermicides
(Los Espermaticidas)

1. Spermicides come in the form of jellies, creams, foam or suppositories.

Los espermaticidas vienen en la forma de jaleas, cremas, espuma o supositorios.

2. Spermicides kill sperm before they enter the uterus and fertilize the egg.
Los espermaticidas matan los espermas antes de que entren en el útero y fecunden al óvulo.

3. It is best to use spermicides with a condom and/or a diaphragm.
Es mejor usar los espermaticidas con el condón y/o el diafragma.

4. You can buy spermicides without a prescription.
Se puede comprar los espermaticidas sin receta.

E. The Condom
(El Condón)

1. The condom is a thin sleeve that adjusts on the penis to trap the semen.
El condón es una funda delgada que se ajusta al pene para atrapar el semen.

2. Condoms protect against A.I.D.S. and other sexually-transmitted diseases.
Los condones previenen contra el S.I.D.A. y otras enfermedades transmitidas sexualmente.

3. They are cheap and available without prescription.
Son baratos y accesibles sin receta.

F. Depo-Provera
(inyección anticoncepcional)

1. Depo-Provera is an injectable method of contraception that protects against pregnancy for a total of three months.
Depo-Provera es un método anticoncepcional inyectable que protege del embarazo por un total de tres meses.

2. It does not contain estrogen.
No contiene estrógeno.

3. It can be used by breast feeding mothers.
Puede ser usado por madres que lactan a sus bebés.

4. Birth control protection begins as soon as the first injection is administered.
Los efectos de control de la natalidad comienzan tan pronto como recibe la primera inyección.

G. Ortho Evra
(El Parcho Anticonceptivo)

1. Ortho Evra is a highly effective contraceptive patch.
Ortho Evra es un parcho anticonceptivo altamente efectivo.

2. The patch is attached to the skin weekly to avoid pregnancy.
Se coloca el parcho sobre la piel semanalmente para prevenir el embarazo.

3. The patch has to be changed weekly, for a period of three weeks.
Hay que cambiar el parcho una vez a la semana durante tres semanas consecutivas.

4. The fourth week is free of the patch.
La cuarta semana es libre del parcho.

5. You can expect your menstruation a few days after removing the third patch.
Puede esperar su menstruación unos pocos días después de quitarse el tercer parcho.

6. The patch should be changed on the same day each week.
El parcho debe ser cambiado el mismo día cada semana.

7. You can use the patch on the behind, the stomach, the shoulder blades, or the upper part of the arm.
Se puede usar el parcho o en los glúteos, el abdomen, la escápula, ó la parte superior de los brazos.

8. The patch is almost one hundred percent effective in preventing pregnancy if used correctly.
El parcho es casi cien por ciento seguro para prevenir el embarazo, si es usada correctamente.

H. Female Sterilization
(Esterilización Femenina)

1. This is a simple operation that seals the fallopian tubes and prevents the union of the egg and the sperm.
Es una operación fácil que cierra las trompas de falopio para prevenir la unión del óvulo y la esperma.

2. Sterilization is a permanent, non-reversible operation.
La esterilización es una operación permanente e irreversible.

3. It is almost 100% effective in preventing pregnancy.
Es casi cien por ciento seguro para prevenir el embarazo.

4. It is a good option for a couple that is sure that they have had all the children they want.
Es una buena alternativa para las parejas que están seguros que ya tienen todos los niños que desean.

I. Vasectomy
(Vasectomía)

1. It is a simple operation in which the doctor cuts and ties or seals the tubes that transport the sperm from the testicles to the penis.
Es una operación sencilla en donde el doctor corta, amarra o sella los tubos que llevan la esperma de los testículos al pene.

2. The operation can be done in the doctor's office in less than a half an hour.
La operación se puede hacer en la oficina del doctor en menos de media hora.

3. The operation is easier and more economical than female sterilization.
La operación es más fácil y económica que la esterilización de la mujer.

4. It is 100% effective in preventing pregnancy eight weeks after the operation.
Es cien por ciento seguro para prevenir el embarazo ocho semanas después de la operación.

J. Natural Family Planning
(Planificación Natural de la Familia)

1. This method is based on observing a woman's cycle to determine ovulation.
Este método se basa en la observación del ciclo de la mujer para determinar la ovulación.

2. During ovulation, intercourse is avoided or another method of contraception is used.
Durante la ovulación o se evitan las relaciones sexuales o se usa otro método.

3. This method requires education and commitment from both partners.
Este método requiere educación y compromiso de los dos.

WELL WOMAN CARE AND GYNECOLOGY
The STD Interview

1. Do you have pain in the lower part of the abdomen?
¿Tiene dolor en la parte baja del abdomen?

2. Do you have pain or burning when you urinate?
¿Tiene dolor o ardor al orinar?

3. Do you have unusual vaginal secretions?
¿Tiene secreciones vaginales poco comunes?

4. Do you bleed after having sexual relations?
¿Sangra luego de tener relaciones sexuales?

5 Do you bleed between menstrual periods?
¿Sangra entre períodos menstruales?

6. Do you have pain during intercourse?
¿Tiene dolor durante la relación sexual?

7. Do you have itching in the genital area?
¿Tiene picazón de la región genital?

8. Do you have a genital sore, lesion or wart?
¿Tiene alguna herida, lesión o verruga en la región genital?

9. Has your weight changed recently?
¿Ha cambiado de peso recientemente?

10. How many pounds have you lost / gained?
¿Cuántas libras ha perdido / aumentado?

11. Do you have as much energy as usual?
¿Tiene tanta energía como siempre?

12. Have you had fever? Night sweats?
¿Ha tenido fiebre? ¿Sudoraciones durante la noche?

13. How long have you had these symptoms?
¿Por cuánto tiempo ha tenido estos síntomas?

14. Does the man with whom you had sexual relations also have these symptoms?
¿Tiene los mismos síntomas el hombre con quien ha tenido relaciones sexuales?

15. When was the last time you had sex?
¿Cuándo fue la última vez que tuvo relaciones sexuales?

16. Did your partner use a condom?
¿Usó su compañero un condón?

17. Have you ever been tested for Syphilis? Gonorrhea? Herpes? AIDS? HIV?
¿Le hicieron antes una prueba para detectar la sífilis? la gonorrea? el herpes? el SIDA? el VIH?

18. Were the results positive or negative?
¿Fueron los resultados positivos o negativos?

19. Were you treated?
¿Recibió tratamiento?

20. You have contracted a Sexually Transmitted Disease (STD).
Usted se ha infectado de una Enfermedad de Transmisión Sexual (ETS).

21. Clamidia is the most common of the Sexually Transmitted Diseases.
La clamidia es la más común de las Enfermedades de Transmisión Sexual.

22. Clamidia is transmitted through sexual contact with an infected person.
La clamidia se transmite a través del contacto sexual con una persona infectada.

23. If this disease is not treated, the consequences could be serious.
Si no se trata esta enfermedad, las consecuencias podrían ser serias.

24. It can cause infertility.
Puede causar infertilidad.

25. It can cause sterility.
Puede causar esterilidad.

26. It can cause ectopic pregnancies.
Puede causar embarazos ectópicos.

27. It can cause Inflammatory Pelvic Disease.
Puede causar la Enfermedad Pélvica Inflamatoria (EPI).

28. Inflammatory Pelvic Disease is an infection of the uterus, Fallopian tubes and ovaries.
La Enfermedad Pélvica Inflamatoria es una infección del útero, las trompas de Falopio y los ovarios.

WELL WOMAN CARE AND GYNECOLOGY
Gynecological Cancer Screening

1. Have you ever had breast cancer?
¿Ha tenido alguna vez cáncer del seno?

2. When was the last time you had a mammogram?
¿Cuándo fue la última vez que le hicieron una mamografía?

3. You should have a mammogram every one to two years.
Debe hacerse una mamografía cada uno a dos años.

4. Early detection is the key to surviving and successfully treating breast cancer.
La detección temprana es la clave para sobrevivir y tratar con éxito el cáncer del seno.

5. Have you ever had a biopsy of the breast?
¿Le han hecho alguna vez una biopsia del seno?

6. What was the result?
¿Cuál fue el resultado?

7. Is there a history of breast cancer in your family?
¿Hay historial de cáncer del seno en su familia?

8. Who was diagnosed with cancer?
¿Quién ha sido diagnosticado con cáncer?

9. When was your last breast examination?
¿Cuándo fue la última vez que le examinaron los senos?

10. Do you know how to examine your breasts?
¿Sabe examinarse los senos?

11. You need to examine your breasts monthly.
Necesita examinar los senos cada mes.

12. I will show you how.
Le enseñaré como examinarse.

13. Is there a history of cancer of the reproductive system in your family?
¿Hay historial de cáncer del sistema reproductor en su familia?

14. Has your uterus been removed?
¿Le han sacado la matriz?

15. Have you ever been diagnosed with ovarian cancer?
¿Ha sido diagnosticado con cáncer del ovario?

16. Has one of your ovaries been removed? Two ovaries?
¿Le han sacado un ovario? ¿Dos ovarios?

17. When was the last time you had a test for cervical cancer?
¿Cuándo fue la última vez que le hicieron la prueba de cáncer del cérvix?

18. Was it normal?
¿Salió normal?

19. Have you had an abnormal pap smear in the past?
¿Ha tenido una prueba de cáncer anormal en el pasado?

20. You need to do this test every year.
Necesita hacer esta prueba todos los años.

21. Have you ever been diagnosed with endometriosis?
¿Ha sido diagnosticado con la endometriosis?

22. Endometriosis is a condition that occurs when the endometrial lining grows outside the uterus.
La endometriosis es una condición que ocurre cuando el tejido endometrial crece fuera del útero.

23. Once outside the uterus, the endometrial tissue can form very painful tumors.
Una vez fuera del útero, el tejido endometrial puede formar tumores que causan gran dolor.

24. Do you have a lot of pain when you menstruate?
¿Tiene mucho dolor durante la menstruación?

25. Do you have heavy or irregular bleeding?
¿Experimenta mucho sangrado o sangrado irregular?

26. Do you feel a lot of pressure or chronic pelvic pain?
¿Siente mucha presión o dolores pélvicos crónicos?

27. We can make a precise diagnosis through a procedure called laparoscopy.
Podemos realizar un diagnóstico preciso mediante un procedimiento denominado laparoscopia.

28. Superficial tumors can be eliminated through incision, electric current or laser.
Los tumores superficiales pueden ser eliminados mediante incisión, corriente eléctrico o rayos láser.

29. In extreme cases, a hysterectomy may be necessary.
En los casos extremos, puede que sea necesaria la histerectomía.

30. In many cases, endometriosis can be treated with hormones.
En muchos casos, se puede tratar la endometriosis con hormonas.

31. Uterine fibroids are the most common type of tumor found in the female pelvis.
Los fibromas uterinos son el tipo de tumor más común que se encuentra en la pelvis femenina.

32. They are usually benign.
Usualmente son benignos.

33. With time, diseases of the uterus can change into cancer.
Con el tiempo, las enfermedades del cuello uterino pueden convertirse en cáncer.

34. That is why early intervention and treatment are so important.
Por eso la intervención y el tratamiento temprano son tan importantes.

WELL WOMAN CARE AND GYNECOLOGY
Menopause

1. Menopause is that time in a woman's life when she stops with menstruation.
La menopausia es la parte de la vida de una mujer cuando cesa de tener la menstruación.

2. Menopause marks the natural end of her fertile years.
La menopausia marca el final natural de los años fértiles.

3. Have you noted any changes in your menstruation?
¿Ha notado algún cambio en la menstruación?

4. Have you had irregular periods?
¿Ha tenido menstruaciones irregulares?

5. Have you experienced memory lapses or forgetfulness?
¿Ha experimentado alguna falta de memoria o despiste?

6. Have you been more irritable lately? Nervous? Depressed?
¿Ha estado más irritable últimamente? ¿Nerviosa? ¿Deprimida?

7. Have you had insomnia?
¿Ha tenido insomnio?

8. Do you have hot flashes?
¿Ha tenido sensaciones de calor repentino?

9. Is intercourse painful for you?
¿Es doloroso tener relaciones sexuales?

10. Where does it hurt you? The vagina? The stomach?
¿Dónde le duele? ¿La vagina? ¿El estómago?

11. Is your vagina dry during intercourse?
¿Está seca la vagina cuando tiene relaciones sexuales?

12. You may need to use a lubricant with intercourse.
Puede que necesite usar un lubricante cuando tenga relaciones sexuales.

13. Lack of hormone production in menopause can make the vagina dry.
Falta de producción de hormonas durante la menopausia puede causar resequedad en la vagina.

14. Intercourse can become uncomfortable.
Las relaciones sexuales pueden llegar a ser incómodas.

15. Sometimes it helps if you touch or kiss each other before intercourse.
A veces ayuda si ustedes se tocan o se besan antes de hacer el amor.

16. These all are symptoms of menopause.
Son todos síntomas de la menopausia.

17. Hormone Replacement Therapy can help to ease the symptoms of menopause.
La Terapia de Reemplazo Hormonal puede ayudar a aliviar los síntomas de la menopausia.

18. Despite signs of menopause, you can still become pregnant.
A pesar de los signos de la menopausia, todavía puede quedar embarazada.

19. Endometriosis is a condition that occurs when the endometrial lining grows outside the uterus.
La endometriosis es una condición que ocurre cuando el tejido endometrial crece fuera del útero.

20. You need to protect yourself if you are having sexual relations.
Necesita protegerse si está teniendo relaciones sexuales.

21. Were you ever hurt in the abdomen?
¿Se ha lastimado el abdomen alguna vez?

22. Has anyone mistreated you physically or sexually?
¿Le ha maltrado alguien físicamente o sexualmente?

23. Does anyone hit you? Kick you?
¿Le ha pegado alguien? ¿Le han dado patadas?

24. Are you afraid?
¿Tiene miedo?

25. I will try not to make you uncomfortable.
Trataré de no incomodarla.

26. Will you allow me to examine you?
¿Me permite examinarle?

27. The pelvic exam is essential for the early detection of cancer or infection.
El examen pélvico es esencial para la pronta detección de cáncer o una infección.

28. Would you please wait here. Outside.
Por favor, me hace el favor de esperar aquí. Afuera.

WELL WOMAN CARE AND GYNECOLOGY
Language Activities and Study Guide

Instructions: Set your own timeframe for the following activities. It is recommended that a beginning learner allow three months for this unit, dedicating approximately 30 minutes a day to the goal of learning Spanish for well woman care.

Unit 6 Begin Date: _____
Projected End Date: _____

A. Key Phrases

Listen to the phrases presented on pages 194-216 of the text on the audio program. These phrases will help you to obtain and impart information relevant to gynecological care. Repeat each phrase after the instructor in Spanish. Try to imitate the pronunciation as closely as you can. Listen for the vocabulary you already know. This will give you confidence as you begin to recognize familiar words.

When you are confident of the pronunciation, select 90 phrases that you find most useful to you. Place each phrase on a separate index card. Memorize one phrase per day until you have learned all 90 phrases (1 phrase per day x 90 days = 3 months).

B. **Targeted Grammar and Structure: The Key Verb Tener**

There is probably no other verb in Spanish that is as useful in perinatal situations as the verb "tener" (to have).

Conjugation of Tener in the Present Tense:

Yo tengo (I have)
Tú tienes (You have)
El, ella, usted tiene (He, She or It has)
Nosotros tenemos (We have)
Ustedes tienen (You have)

Activity #1: Fill in the blank with the correct conjugation of the verb "tener."

¿ _____ (usted) dolor en la parte baja del abdomen?
¿ _____ (su papá) dolor o ardor al orinar?
¿ _____ (tú) secreciones vaginales poco comunes?
¿ _____ (usted) dolor durante la relación sexual?

¿ _____ (ustedes) picazón de la región genital?

¿ _____ (su novia) alguna herida, lesión o verruga en la región genital?

¿ _____ (ustedes) tanta energía como siempre?

¿ _____ (tú) muchos compañeros?

¿ _____ (nosotros) mucho miedo.

¿ _____ (yo) tengo historial de cáncer de seno en mi familia.

C. **Language Learning Activity #1: Family Planning and Contraception**

Situation: Janira González and José Ramírez have come to your office for advice about birth control. They have two children. Janira is thirty years old and José is thirty-two. Janira and José have decided that they do not want any more children and are interested in a more permanent method of birth control. Counsel Janira and José on their options following the model dialogue.

Enfermera: Buenos días. ¿En qué los puedo ayudar?

José: Queremos saber como podemos evitar otro embarazo.

Enfermera: ¿Piensan tener más hijos?

José: No, no queremos más. Tenemos la parejita.

Enfermera: ¿Usa actualmente algún método para evitar el embarazo?

José: Si, usamos.

Enfermera: ¿Cuál método prefiere?

Janira: Me ponen una inyección cada tres meses.

Enfermera: ¿Te gusta este método?

José: No mucho. A veces se le olvida ir a la clínica.

Enfermera: ¿Quieren cambiar a otro método?

José: Queremos algo más fácil, o sea, más permanente. Ella puede esterilizarse ¿verdad?

Enfermera: Sí, se puede, pero hay otros métodos que son eficaces, duraderos y reversibles. Por ejemplo, hay un aparato que se llama el D.I.U. Da protección hasta por diez años.

Janira: Pero, estamos decididos a no tener más hijos. ¿No sería más fácil la esterilización?

Enfermera: Pues, es una opción. Pero, esta operación es permanente y no reversible. Hay que pensarlo bien.

José: Si, estamos decididos. La vida es muy dura. No queremos más hijos.

Janira: ¿No hay una operación para el hombre también?

José. Yo no. No me van a tocar nada.

Enfermera: La operación para esterilizar al hombre se llama la vasectomía. Es una operación sencilla que se puede hacer en la oficina del doctor en menos de media hora.

José: Mejor que se opere ella.

Janira: Está bien. No me importa. Solo quiero evitar tener más hijos.

José: ¿Es complicada la operación?

Enfermera: No, la operación es sencilla.

Janira: ¿Tendría que pasar la noche en el hospital?

Enfermera: No es necesario pasar la noche. Es una cirugía ambulatoria.

José: Pues, lo vamos a pensar. Muchas gracias por sus consejos.

Enfermera: A la orden. Llévense los folletitos que explican ambos la vasectomía y la esterilización femenina. Avísenme cualquier cosa que decidan.

D. **Language Learning Activity #2:
Encuesta Sobre el Riesgo de Cáncer**

The following activity is a model form to identify women at risk for breast or cervical cancer. Interview one of your patients using this form, or create one of your own!

1. ¿Ha tenido alguna vez cáncer de seno? __ sí __ no

2. ¿Cuándo fue la última vez que le hicieron una mamografía? _____.

3. ¿Le han hecho alguna vez una biopsia de seno? ____ sí ____ no (Una biopsia de seno es cuando el médico extrae tejido de su seno para hacer pruebas para el cáncer).

4. Si la respuesta es sí, ¿cuántas biopsias de seno se le han hecho? _____

5. ¿Cuáles fueron los resultados?
_____

6. ¿Le dijo su médico alguna vez que una de sus biopsias mostraba un estado precanceroso?_ sí _ no

7. Hay historial de cáncer de seno o del sistema reproductor en su familia? ____ sí ____ no

8. ¿Quién ha sido diagnosticado con cáncer de seno?
_____

9. ¿Quién ha sido diagnosticado con cáncer del sistema reproductor? _____

10. ¿Sabe examinarse los senos? ____ sí ____ no
¿Lo hace? ____ sí ____ no

11. ¿Ha tenido alguna vez cáncer del sistema reproductor? ____ sí ____ no

12. ¿Le han sacado la matriz? ____ sí ____ no
¿Los ovarios? ____ sí ____ no

13. ¿Cuándo fue la última vez que le hicieron la prueba papanicolau? (la prueba de cáncer del cérviz)
_____

14. ¿Salió normal? ____ sí ____ no

Cultural Reading
Marianismo and Machismo:
How do these cultural values affect gynecological decisions?

As you know, the Hispanic culture is as varied as our own, with a wide variety of individual traditions and local as opposed to national belief systems. But, just as we can define our culture by some mutually-agreed-upon generalizations, so can we with the Hispanic culture. There are some generally-accepted historical values which have been handed down from generation to generation across the diverse cultures of Latin America. Two of those values are *marianismo* and *machismo,* which are really just two sides of the same coin. The following information has been taken from the book, <u>The María Paradox</u>, written by Rosa María Gil.

So much has been written about *machismo* both within and outside the Latino community that the word has entered the English language as a synonym for oppressive male supremacy. However, *machismo* would not survive were it not for the other side of the coin, which is equally rigidly enforced and deeply woven into the fabric of Hispanic life.

The other side of the coin of machismo is called *marianismo*. *Marianismo* defines the ideal role of the Hispanic woman, taking as its role model none other than the Virgin Mary. *Marianismo* is defined by the following characteristics:

Marianismo: The Traditional Female Hispanic Role is:
- self-sacrificing, pure and virginal
- patient and forgiving
- dependent
- accepting of infidelities and\or abuses
- unwilling to change those things which make her unhappy

Marianismo supports the belief that:
- any marriage is better than no marriage at all
- virginity is important to securing a good marriage
- the role of wife and mother is of great personal and social value
- sex is for making babies, not pleasure
- it is unacceptable to seek help or discuss personal problems outside the home

While *Marianismo* defines the ideal women, *Machismo* defines a socially learned and reinforced set of behaviors in Latino society which men are expected to follow.

Machismo is considered the sum total of what a man should be, and is defined by the following characteristics:

Machismo: The Traditional Male Hispanic role is:

- gentleman *(caballero)*
- autocratic decision maker
- ladies' man *(mujeriego)*
- protector of wife and family

Machismo supports the belief that:

- men have options; women have duties
- a man's place is in the world, woman's in the home
- men give the orders, women obey
- sex is for pleasure, and if a wife is sick, pregnant, or unwilling to fulfill her conjugal duty, it is a husband's right to seek satisfaction elsewhere
- An unfaithful man is a true man
- Virginity in a future wife is highly valued and usually expected.

The old world values of *machismo* and *marianismo* are slowly losing their hold on Hispanic society in general, but remain very much alive among groups in the lower socio-economic and educational levels. These traditional behaviors can still be seen, even among young, childbearing couples today.

New values are replacing old stereotypes and the Hispanic family is evolving into a modern role of greater equality and more democratic interaction. However, like any change, the transition from old world to new world values is a process of adaptation and acculturation. Of interest to us as childbirth professionals, however, is how these cultural values affect gynecological decisions of Hispanic women.

How cultural values affect gynecological decisions:

- many Latinas will not use a tampon for fear of rupturing the hymen
- some Latinas have even gone so far as to undergo reconstructive surgery to reconstruct the hymen and create the illusion of virginity for their future spouse.

"I wanted to make him believe that I had never had a sexual relation with another man. In my country the men are *machistas,* and even though they say that they will love you the same, the respect is not there," says Maria, a 33 year old Columbian woman who had reconstructive surgery of the hymen.

Latinas are often caught between two worlds, one which teaches that a young woman should be sexually active to please her man, and the other that teaches that because of the machismo inherent in her own culture, she should be a virgin when she marries to please her husband.

- Many Latinas are uncomfortable using diaphragms because they are shy about touching themselves
- Because of the allowed promiscuity of the Latin male, Hispanic women are at a high risk of becoming infected with HIV or other sexually-transmitted diseases.

The following information is taken from an article that appeared in Time Magazine called *"Amores Que Matan: El Letal Cóctel de SIDA y Machismo Amenaza a las Mujeres Latinoamericanas."* The author, Silvana Paternostro, begins by stating that . . .

"Those woman considered immune to the HIV virus are those that should actually be most worried. Prostitutes will usually protect themselves while housewives and married woman, precisely because they are conservative and respectful, are more vulnerable than we imagine."

"In the last ten years, Latin woman have become the principal victims of HIV, 70% of them having contracted the virus through heterosexual relations. The majority are infected by their husbands. Why: For one simple reason. Machismo, which perpetuates the sexual inequality between men and women."

"It is socially acceptable and even expected that Latin-American men have the right to a sexual life outside of the home. In the *machista* mentality, the unfaithful man is more of a man. Their women should not only support this position but also pretend that they don't know about it. If they do know about it, they should suffer in silence.

Many will ask, given the reality of this *machista* culture, is it reasonable to expect that the Latin male wear a condom? The author answers as follows:

"Attempts to get Latin men to use condoms will most likely be unsuccessful. Why? Once again, el *machismo*."

"Latin men tend to only wear condoms with *putas* (prostitutes), who are considered *sucio* (dirty), or with women at the beginning of a relationship."

Once you become his *novia*, girlfriend, or his wife, it is not necessary for him to wear a condom. If you ask him to wear one, he may become suspicious."

Pronunciation Guide

I. The Vowels

As in English, the vowels are *a, e, i, o, u.*

A The "a" is similar to the "a" in "father."
E The "e" is similar to the "a" in "cake", but shorter.
I The "i" is similar to the "ee" in "see", but shorter.
O The "o" is similar to the "o" in "go," but shorter.
U The "u" is similar to the "oo" in "boot."

II. The Consonants

The pronunciation of most Spanish consonants is close to that of English. However, Spanish sounds are never exactly the same as English sounds. For this reason the following rules are offered as guidelines.

A. The pronunciation of these consonants is almost identical in Spanish and English.

CH The "ch" sounds like the English "ch" as in "chile."
F   The "f" sounds like the English "f" as in "fountain."
L   The "l" sounds like the English "l" as in "lamp."
M   The "m" sounds like the English "m" as in "map."
N   The "n" sounds like the English "n" as in "no."
P   The "p" sounds like the English "p" as in "patio."
S   The "s" sounds like the English "s" as in "soup."
T   The "t" sounds like the English "t" as in "tomato."

B. These consonants have more than one pronunciation in Spanish, depending on the letter that follows.

C The "c" before "a," "o," or "u" is pronounced like the English "k" as in "car."
   The "c" before "e," or "i" is pronounced like the English "s" as in "circus."
G The "g" before "a," "o," or "u" is hard, like the English "g" in "got."
   The "g" before "e," or "i" is pronounced like the English "h" as in "have."
X The "x " before a vowel is pronounced like the English "ks," as in "taxi."
   The "x" before a consonant is pronounced like the English "s" as in "Sam."

C. The sounds of these Spanish consonants are almost identical to sounds in English that are represented by different letters.

Q The "q" is pronounced like the English "k" when followed by "ue," or "ui."
Z The "z" is pronounced like the English "s" as in "sent."

D. The sounds of these Spanish consonants are similar to English sounds that are represented by different letters.

D   The "d" is similar to the "th" in "father."
J   The "j" is similar to the "h" in "help."
LL The "ll" is similar to the "y" in "yes."
N   The "n" is similar to the "ny" in "canyon."

E. These Spanish sounds have no close or exact equivalents in English.

B,V The "b" and "v" are similar to the English "b" but softer. Lips do not close tight, but rather touch and release. There is no difference between the "b" and "v" in Spanish.
R   The "r" is a single tap of the tongue.
RR   The "rr" is strongly trilled.

H   The "h" is silent in Spanish.

III. Syllabification and Dipthongs

When two vowels come together in a syllable to form one sound, it is called a dipthong. The following are the dipthongs in Spanish:

"ia" sounds like "yah" in English: familiar, fiado, malaria.
"ua" sounds like "wa" in "wander:" agua, estatua, enjuagar.
"ai" sounds like "ie" in "pie:" caigo, paisaje, sainete.
"au" sounds like the "ou" in "house:" aunque, gaucho, pausa
"ie" sounds like "ye" in "yellow:" ciego, piel, niebla.
"ue" sounds like the word "way": bueno, duele, muela.
"ei," "ey" sounds like the "ay" in "hay:" peine, rey, seis.
"eu" has no real equivalent in English. Combine Spanish "e" with "u": terapeuta
"io" sounds like the "yo" in "yoga": radio, secundario.
"uo" sounds like the "uo" in "quota:" duodecimo, cuota.
"oi," "oy" sounds like the "oy" in "boy": boina, oigo.
"ui," "uy" sounds like the word "we:" cuidado, muy, suizo.
"iu," "yu" sounds like the word "you:" ciudad, diuretico.

IV. Stress and Accent

1) If a word ends in a vowel, "n," or "s," the stress is on the next to last syllable.
   Example: vaso, hablan, pesos

2) If a word ends in a consonant other than "n" or "s" the stress is on the last syllable.
   Example: comer, doctor, alimentar

3) Any deviation from this rule is indicated by a written accent mark.
   Example: papá, inglés, simpático

Glossary

abdominal pain: *dolor abdominal*
abortion: *aborto provocado*
accident: *accidente*
acidity: *acidez*
addiction: *adicción*
afraid, to be: *tener miedo*
AIDS: *SIDA*
alcohol: *alcohol*
alcoholic beverages: *bebidas alcohólicas*
allergy: *alergia:*
analgesics: *analgésicos*
anemia: *anemia*
anesthesia: *anestesia*
anesthesiologist: *anestesiólogo*
anesthetics: *anestéticos*
ankle: *el tobillo*
antibiotics: *antibióticos*
anus: *el ano*
anxiety: *ansiedad*
appendicitis: *apendicitis*
appetite: *apetito*
appointment: *cita*
apnea: *apnea*
areola: *areola*
arm: *el brazo*
armpit: *la axila*
arthritis: *artritis*
asthma: *asma*
aunt: *tía*
avoid, to: *evitar*
backache: *dolor de espalda*
bandage: *el vendaje*
band-aid: *curita*
baptize, to: *bautizar*

bathroom: *el baño*
bed: *la cama*
bedpan: *el pato, la chata*
benign: *benigno*
bilirubin: *bilirrubina*
biopsy: *biopsia*
birth, the: *el nacimiento*
birth canal: *canal de nacimiento*
birth date: *fecha de nacimiento*
birth defect: *defecto de nacimiento*
bladder: *la vejiga*
bladder infection: *infección de la vejiga*
blanket: *frisa, cobija*
bleed, to: *sangrar*
bleeding: *sangrado*
blind: *ciego*
blood: *sangre*
blood analysis: *análisis de sangre*
blood clots: *coágulos de sangre*
blood pressure: *presión sanguínea*
blood transfusion: *transfusión de sangre*
blow, to: *soplar*
blurred vision: *vista borrosa*
body: *el cuerpo*
bone: *el hueso*
bottle: *el biberón, el bibi*
bottlefeed: *dar el biberón*
boyfriend: *novio*
bra: *sostén, brassiere*
bradycardia: *bradicardia*
breakfast: *el desayuno*
breast: *el seno*
breast feed, to: *dar pecho, lactar*
breast pump: *bomba de succión para senos*
breathe, to: *respirar*
breech: *de nalgas*
broken bone: *hueso roto*
bronchitis: *bronquitis*
brother: *hermano*
bruise: *moretón*

burn, a: *una quemadura*
buttocks: *las nalgas*
caffeine: *cafeína*
calcium: *calcio*
call bell: *el timbre*
calories: *calorías*
calves: *pantorillas*
cancer: *cáncer*
capsule: *cápsula*
carbonated water: *agua carbonatada*
card: *tarjeta*
cardiac monitor: *monitor cardiaco*
car seat: *asiento de carro*
cash; *efectivo*
cast: *yeso*
catheter: *catéter*
centimeters: *centímetros*
cereals: *cereales*
cervix: *cerviz*
cesarean: *cesárea*
chest: *el pecho*
chicken pox: *varicela*
children: *hijos*
chills: *escalofríos*
chin: *la barbilla*
cholera: *cólera*
cholesterol: *colesterol*
cigarrettes: *cigarillos*
cigars: *cigaros*
circumcise, to: *circuncidar*
circumcision: circuncisión
clots: *coágulos*
colic: *cólico*
coffee: *café*
cold, a: *resfriado, catarro*
colostrum: *calostro*
complications: *complicaciones*
condom: *condón*
congenital defects: *defectos congenitales*
consent: *consentimiento*

constipation: *estreñimiento*
contact lenses: *lentes de contacto*
contagious: *contagiosa*
contraceptives: *anticonceptivos*
contraction: *contracción*
contusion: *contusión*
convulse, to: *convulsar*
convulsions: *convulsiones*
copayment: *co-pago*
cough, a: *tos*
crackers: *galletas saladas*
cramps: *calambres*
crib: *la cuna*
crib death: *la muerte de cuna*
critical: *crítico*
crown, to: *coronar*
crutches: *muletas*
cyst: *quiste*
deaf: *sordo*
death: *la muerte*
deductible: *deducible*
deep breathing: *respiración profunda*
delivery: *el parto*
demerol: *demerol*
dentures: *dentaduras postizas*
dependents: *dependientes*
depressed: *deprimido,a*
depression: *depresión*
diabetes: *diabetes*
diagnosis: *diagnóstico*
diaper: *el pañal*
diaphragm: *el diafragma*
diarrhea: *diarrea*
die, to: *morir*
dilation: *la dilatación*
dinner: *la cena*
diptheria: *diftéria*
discharge: *descarga*
discomfort: *malestar*
disinfect: *desinfectar*

dislocated: *dislocado*
dizziness: *mareos*
dizzy: mareado, a
doctor: *doctor/a*
Downs Syndrome: *Síndrome de Downs*
drool, to: *babear*
drugs: *drogas*
drunk: *borracho, a*
due date: *fecha de parto*
dust: *polvo*
earache: *dolor de oido*
eat, to: *comer*
effacement: *el borramiento del cerviz*
elbow: *el codo*
electrocardiogram: *electrocardiograma*
emergency: *emergencia*
enema: *enema*
English: *inglés*
epidural: *epidural*
epilepsy: *epilepsia*
episiotomy: *episiotomía / el corte*
estrogen: *estrógeno*
examine, to: *examinar*
exercises: *ejercicios*
exhale, to: *exhalar*
eye glasses: *espuejuelos, anteojos*
eyes: *los ojos*
face down: *boca abajo*
fallopian tubes: *las trompas de falopio*
family: *la familia*
fat: *grasa*
father: *padre*
fatigue: *cansancio*
feet: *los pies*
fertile: *fértil*
fertility: *fertilidad*
fetal monitor: *el monitor del feto*
fever: *fiebre*
fill out, to: *llenar*
fingers: *los dedos*

fireman: *bombero*
fist: *el puño*
flu, the: *la gripe, la monga*
focal point: *punto focal*
food: *alimento*
forceps: *fórceps*
form: *formulario*
fracture: *fractura*
fresh air: *aire fresco*
fried foods: *frituras*
friend: *amigo/a*
fruits: *frutas*
gall bladder: *la vesícula biliar*
genital infection: *infección genital*
genital warts: *verrugas genitales*
genitals: *los genitales*
German Measles: *Rubeola*
girlfriend: *novia*
give birth, to: *dar a luz*
gland: *glándula*
Glaucoma: *glaucoma*
Gonorrhea: *gonorrea*
gown: *la bata*
grains: *granos*
grandfather: *abuelo*
grandmother; *abuela*
groin: la ingle
grow, to: *crecer*
gunshot wound: *herida de bala*
hands: *las manos*
hay fever: *fiebre del heno*
head: *la cabeza*
headache: *dolor de cabeza*
health: *salud*
healthy: *sano*
hearing aid: *aparato del oido*
heart: *corazón*
heart attack: *ataque cardiaco, infarto*
heartbeat: *latidos del corazón*
heartburn: *acidez*

heart disease: *enfermedad cardiaca*
heart monitor: *monitor cardiaco*
heater: *calentador*
hemorrhage: hemorragia
hemorrhoids: *hemorroides*
hepatitis: *hepatitis*
hernia: *hernia*
Herpes: *herpes*
high blood pressure: *presión alta*
hips: *las caderas*
hit, to: *pegar*
hoarse: *ronca*
hood: *capucha*
hormones: *hormonas*
hospital room: *el cuarto*
husband: *esposo*
hypertension: *hipertensión*
hysterectomy: *histerectomía*
ice: *hielo*
ice chips: *pedacitos de hielo*
ice pack: *bolsa de hielo*
illness: *enfermedad*
immunization: *immunización*
implant: *implante*
incision: *incisión*
income: *ingreso*
increase, to: *aumentar*
incubator: *incubador*
indigestion: *indigestión*
induce, to: *inducir*
infection: *infección*
infertility: *infertilidad*
inflammation: *inflamación*
intervention: *intervención*
inhale, to: *inhalar*
injection: *inyección*
insomnia: *insomnio*
insulin: *insulina*
insurance: *plan médico*
intensive care: *cuidado intensivo*

intestines: *los intestinos*
intubate: *intubar*
iodine: *yodo*
iron pills: *pastillas de hierro*
itching: *picazón*
I.U.D.: *dispositivo intrauterino*
IV: *el suero*
jaundice: *ictericia*
jewlery: *prendas*
joints: *articulaciones*
kidneys: *los riñones*
kidney disease: *enfermedad del riñon*
kidney stones: *piedras en los riñones*
knees: *las rodillas*
labor: *el trabajo de parto*
laboratoy: *laboratorio*
lap: *el regazo, la falda*
latch on, to: *agarrar el seno*
laxatives: *laxantes*
lead poisoning: *envenenamiento del plomo*
legs: *las piernas*
lie down, to: *acostarse*
liver: *el hígado*
Living Will: *Testamento Activo*
lower lip: *el labio inferior*
lubricant: *lubricante*
lump: *masa*
lungs: *los pulmones*
lymph nodes: *nodos linfáticos*
malaria: *malaria*
mammogram: *mamografía*
mask: *mascarilla*
massage: *masaje*
measles: *sarampión*
medical treatment: *tratamiento medico*
medication: *medicamento*
medicine: *medicina*
membranes: *la bolsa de agua / la fuente*
meningitis: *menigitis*
menopause: *menopausia*

menstrual cycle: *la menstruación, la regla*
mental health: *salud mental*
midwife: *partera*
migraine: *migraña*
milk: *leche*
miscarriage: *aborto natural*
mother: *madre*
mother's milk: *la leche materna*
mouth: *la boca*
multivitamin: *multivitamina*
mumps: *páperas*
muscles: *los músculos*
narcotics: *narcóticos*
nausea: *náuseas*
neck: *el cuello*
neonatal: *neonatal*
neonatalogist: *neonatólogo*
nerve damange: *daño a los nervios*
nerves: *nervios*
new born: *recién nacido*
nickname: *apodo*
nipple: *el pezón*
nose: *la nariz*
numb: *adormecida*
nurse: *enfermera/o*
nursery: *la Sala de Recién Nacidos*
nursing bra: *sostén de maternidad*
nutritionist: *nutricionista*
nutritious foods: *alimentos nutritivos*
ointment: *unguento*
operating room: *la Sala de Operaciones*
ounces: *onzas*
ovaries: *los ovarios*
overdose: *dósis excesiva*
ovulation: *ovulación*
oxygen: *oxígeno*
pace maker: *marcapasos*
pain: *dolor*
palpitations: *palpitaciones*
pap smear: *papanicolau, prueba de cáncer*

paralysis: *parálisis*
paramedic: *paramédico*
parasites: *parasitos*
partner: *pareja, compañero*
pastor: *el pastor*
pediatrician: *pedíatra*
pelvis: *la pélvis*
penicillin: *penicilina*
penis: *el pene*
pharmacist: *farmacéutico*
phlegm: *flema*
physical therapist: *terapista física*
pill, the: *la píldora, la pastilla*
pillow: *la almohada*
Pitocin: *pitocina*
placenta: *la placenta*
pneumonia: *pulmonía*
poison: *veneno*
poisoning: *envenenamiento*
police: *la policía*
polio: *polio*
pounds: *libras*
pregnancy: *el embarazo*
pregnancy test: *prueba de embarazo*
pregnant, to be: *estar embarazada*
premature: *prematuro*
prenatal: *prenatal*
prenatal care: *cuidado prenatal*
prenatal vitamins: *vitaminas prenatales*
prescription: *la receta*
prescription medicine: *medicina recetada*
pressure: *presión*
priest: *el sacerdote*
procedures: *procedimientos*
prostate: *próstata*
protein: *proteína*
pulled muscle: *un músculo estirado*
pulse: *el pulso*
push, to: *pujar*
question: *pregunta*

question, to: *preguntar*
rash: *sarpullido*
recovery: *recuperación*
recovery room: *Sala de Recuperación*
rectum: *el recto*
relax, to: *relajarse*
religion: *religión*
remove, to: *quitarse*
respirations: *respiraciones*
respirator: *respiradora*
rest, to: *descansar*
resuscitate: *resucitar*
rheumatic fever: *fiebre reumática*
rub, to: *sobar*
salt: *sal*
salty: *salada*
sanitary pad: *toalla sanitaria*
scale: *la báscula, la pesa, la balanza*
scar: *cicatriz*
scarlet fever: *fiebre escarlata*
secretary: *secretaria*
sedative: *sedante*
seizures: *convulsiones*
sexual disease: *enfermedad sexual*
sexual relations: *relaciones sexuales*
shave, to: *afeitar, rasurar*
sheets: *sábanas*
shortness of breath: *falta de aire*
shoulders: *los hombros*
sick, to be: *estar enfermo/a*
sickness: *enfermedad*
side effects: *efectos secundarios*
sign, to: *firmar*
sister: *hermana*
sit down, to: *sentarse*
sitz bath: *baño de asiento*
skin: *la piel*
small pox: *viruela*
smoke, to: *fumar*
soak, to: *remojar*

snack: *merienda*
social security: *seguridad social*
social worker: *trabajador/a social*
sore: *adolorido*
sour tase: *sabor amargo*
Spanish: *español*
speculum: *espéculo*
sperm: *esperma*
spermacide: *espermaticidas*
spicy foods: *alimentos picantes*
spinal tap: *punción lumbar*
splint: *la tablilla*
spots: *manchas*
sprain: *torcedura*
sprained ankle: *un tobillo torcido*
sputum: *esputo*
stable: *estable*
stabilize, to: *estabilizar*
sterility: *esterilidad*
sterilize: *esterilizar*
stiches: *los puntos*
stiff: *rígido*
stiffen, to: *endurecer*
stimulate, to: *estimular, provocar*
stirrups: *los estribos*
stomach: *el estómago, la barriga*
stools: *escreta, heces*
stretcher: *la camilla*
stroke: *derrame cerebral*
strong: *fuerte*
suicide: *suicidio*
suppository: *supositorio*
support: *apoyo*
surgery: *cirugía*
sweat: *sudor*
sweat, to: *sudar*
swell, to: *hinchar*
swelling: *hinchazón*
swollen: *hinchado*
swollen glands, *glándulas hinchadas*

symptoms: *síntomas*
Syphilis: *sífilis*
tablet: *tableta*
take, to: *tomar*
technician: *técnico*
temperature: *temperatura*
test: *prueba*
Tetanus: *tétano*
thermomenter: *el termómetro*
throat: *la garganta*
toes: *los dedos de los pies*
tongue: *la lengua*
tourniquet: *torniquete*
trachea: *traquea*
tranquilizer: *tranquilizante*
transition: *transición*
treatment: *tratamiento*
tumor: *tumor*
twins: *gemelos, cuates*
typhoid: *tifoídea*
ulcer: *úlcera*
ultrasound: *sonograma*
umbilical cord: *cordón umbilical*
uncle: *tío*
urinate, to: *orinar*
urine: *orina*
urine sample: *una muestra de orina*
uterus: *el útero*
vaccination: *vacuna*
vagina: *vagina*
vaginal bleeding: *sangrado vaginal*
vaginal discharge: *descarga vaginal*
vaginal infection: *infección vaginal*
varicose veins: *venas varicosas*
vasectomy: *vasectomía*
vegetables: *vegetales*
veneral diseas: *enfermedad venerea*
visiting hours: *horas de visita*
visitors: *visitantes*
vital signs: *signos vitales*

vitamins: *vitaminas*
vomitus: *vómitos*
vomit, to: *vomitar*
waist: *la cintura*
wait, to: *esperar*
waiting room: *Sala de Espera*
walk, to: *caminar*
warm towels: *toallas tibias*
water: *agua*
weak: *débil*
wean, to: *destetar*
weigh, to: *pesar*
weight: *peso*
whopping cough: *tosferina*
wound: *herida*
wrist: *muñeca*
witch hazel: *hamamelis*
x ray: *radiografía*

www.ingramcontent.com/pod-product-compliance
Lightning Source LLC
Chambersburg PA
CBHW070336240426
43665CB00045B/2119